Andrews Norton

**The Pentateuch**

And its Relation to the Jewish and Christian Dispensations

Andrews Norton

**The Pentateuch**
*And its Relation to the Jewish and Christian Dispensations*

ISBN/EAN: 9783337026608

Printed in Europe, USA, Canada, Australia, Japan

Cover: Foto ©Lupo / pixelio.de

More available books at **www.hansebooks.com**

# THE PENTATEUCH:

AND ITS RELATION TO

## THE JEWISH AND CHRISTIAN DISPENSATIONS.

By ANDREWS NORTON,

LATE PROFESSOR OF SACRED HISTORY, HARVARD UNIVERSITY, MASS.

EDITED BY

JOHN JAMES TAYLER, B.A.

MEMBER OF THE HISTORICO-THEOLOGICAL SOCIETY OF LEIPSIC, AND PRINCIPAL OF MANCHESTER NEW COLLEGE, LONDON.

LONDON:

LONGMAN, GREEN, LONGMAN, ROBERTS, AND GREEN,

PATERNOSTER ROW.

1863.

LONDON:
PRINTED BY WOODFALL AND KINDER,
ANGEL COURT SKINNER STREET.

# PREFACE.

THE ensuing dissertation is reprinted from a long note appended to the second volume of the late Mr. Norton's elaborate work on the "Genuineness of the Gospels." More than twenty years ago the learned and pious author had adopted and published conclusions respecting the age and authorship of the Pentateuch, substantially identical with those which the appearance of Bishop Colenso's book has recently made the subject of so much eager discussion and hostile criticism. It has been thought that service might be rendered to the cause of religious truth, by bringing Mr. Norton's views once more in a separate form before the public. There must be some powerful reasons to recommend conclusions so much at variance with the popular belief, when we find them forcing themselves on the conviction of independent inquirers in different theological spheres, and, as in the case of the present essay, strenuously maintained by one whose whole cast of mind was cautious and conservative, and who had little sympathy with that German school of thought which is regarded in this country as the special hotbed of critical heresies. Mr. Norton was by temperament disinclined to rash and daring speculation. His mind was essentially logical, and had been well disciplined by habits of exact philological research. That he was not hasty in giving the results of his inquiries to the world, appears from his own confession, that he had committed to writing the substance of his views contained in the following pages, and kept them by him without any essential change in his conclusions, for more than ten years before he submitted them to the public eye. The opinions of such a man on a question of criticism, which lies remote from the popular apprehension and judgment, are entitled, it will be allowed, to a respectful consideration. He has approached this inquiry altogether from the religious side of his nature. His conclusion has been wrung from him not only by the irresistible demands of critical evidence, but even more by his profound reverence for Christianity, and his desire to free it from the disabling liabilities which he conceived an undue estimate of the history of the preceding dispensation had brought upon it. Indeed his devoted attachment to the New Testament seems at times to have made him almost unjust to the Old, and has occasionally involved him in over-subtle and almost sophistical distinctions to dissolve the bond of common ideas and beliefs which are usually thought to connect the two.

On the origin and composition of the Pentateuch and Joshua in the form in which we now possess those books, the views of the editor are in all essential points the same with those of Mr. Norton. Years ago they appeared to him an inevitable inference from the recorded history of the Israelitish commonwealth, and the traces which it exhibits of a gradual development both in its sacerdotal institutions and in the spiritual teachings of its prophets. But he must not be supposed to acquiesce in all the statements, or to sympathize with all the views, which Mr. Norton has interwoven with the exposition of his general theory. On one or two occasions he has ventured to express his dissent in a few brief notes subjoined to the dissertation. He thinks it right to state here in general, that he differs considerably from Mr. Norton in his conception of the source and working of the religious principle in man. He is unable to persuade himself that the whole of man's religious convictions and trusts depends entirely on the miraculously-attested mission of Jesus Christ, and on the simple apprehension by the understanding of the facts involved in that mission. With the sincerest acceptance of Christianity as the religion designed by God for the final healing of our collective humanity, he cannot believe that there has never been any true religion outside its historical forms; but thinks with Paul, and some of the early fathers, that a broader and more genial view of the spiritual nature bestowed on us by God, and the recognition of a divine impulse in those resistless aspirations after the infinite and eternal which characterize the higher thought of man in all religions and all literatures, are indispensable to an adequate appreciation of Christianity itself, and furnish no small portion of the evidence from which its own divinity must be inferred. Thus much the editor may have been permitted to say, to prevent misapprehension respecting himself. Mr. Norton's testimony on the subject of the following treatise is the more valuable, because it comes from a quarter not predisposed to conclusions which it has been found impossible to resist. His essay is here republished without the alteration or omission of a single word. Every man's system of thought forms a whole by itself. We cannot fairly judge of it without seeing it on every side. It would be an unpardonable wrong to the memory of the dead, to reproduce to the world a mutilated image of their ideas, because some of them may appear to certain individuals mistaken or injurious. Wherever the original sources were readily accessible, the author's references have been verified; and the collation has furnished convincing proof of his habitual accuracy and conscientious thoroughness of investigation.

Although the views here avowed may seem startling and offensive to numbers who passively acquiesce in the traditional dogmas of an authoritative Protestantism, those who are at all acquainted with the history of theological opinion, past and present, know perfectly well that they are no novelty, and that men of undoubted piety and profound learning have entertained them. No great weight attaches to Gnostic theories in the second and third centuries, or to the opinions of some Manichæan sectaries in the Middle Ages, because their conclusions are known to have been founded on doctrinal pre-suppositions, and in no sense to have resulted from dispassionate criticism. But with the application of philological learning to theology after the Reformation, inquiry took a new and more healthy direction, and quite as freely, it must be confessed, among Catholics as among Protestants. Carlstadt, a contemporary of Luther, with his characteristic love of paradox, and without stating his reasons at length, declared as early as 1520 that Moses could not be the author of the Pentateuch. In the latter half of the same century Masius, a Catholic jurist, of Brussels, and the author of a commentary much esteemed by the learned on Joshua, avowed, in the preface to that work, his decided conviction that the Pentateuch in its present form was not the production of Moses, but of Ezra or some other later writer, who had modernized some of the ancient names. Hobbes, in his Leviathan, maintained that the Pentateuch was a work concerning Moses, not by Moses,—admitting, however, that he may have been the author of passages of which it is expressly said that he wrote them. Isaac Peyrerius, a French Calvinist minister, who afterwards conformed to the Catholic Church, and died a Jesuit in 1676, in his remarkable work on the Pre-adamites (in which he endeavoured to show that Adam was only the ancestor of the Israelites, and not of the whole human race) advanced the theory that Moses had left journals of the passage from Egypt and written down particular laws, and had prefixed to these a history of the earlier ages, even of that which had preceded Adam; but that these Mosaic autographs had all perished, and that our present books were made up of extracts derived not even immediately from them, and put together at a much later period. Spinoza, the learned philosophical Jew of Amsterdam, in his *Tractatus Theologico-Politicus*, 1670, conjectured that the Pentateuch and the other historical books of the Old Testament were reduced into their present form by Ezra, who first wrote Deuteronomy and then the other four books of the Pentateuch, and attached Deuteronomy to them; and that what is defective and disconnected in these books, arose from the fact that Ezra was prevented by death from putting his last hand to the work, and that after his death it still underwent many alterations.

So far the controversy had been left very much in the hands of Jesuits and laymen. Towards the end of the seventeenth century appeared the celebrated *Histoire Critique du vieux Testament*, by the Père Simon, which gave a new impulse to critical inquiries. Simon ascribes to Moses himself the writing down of the Laws, but supposes that he had appointed certain public annalists, after the manner of the Egyptians, to record the contemporary history; and that out of the different memorials of these annalists, who wrote their respective portions without concert, as well as from the Mosaic Law-book itself, our existing Pentateuch was compiled, but in a manner so confused that it is no longer possible to discriminate the proper Mosaic elements from foreign and later additions. Simon conceived that the narratives and genealogies contained in Genesis had been taken by Moses from other written documents and oral traditions. These bold speculations of the Père Simon called forth a corresponding movement in a section of the Protestant Church. Le Clerc, then a Professor in the Academy of the Remonstrants at Amsterdam, published a series of observations on the work of Simon in the well-known *Sentimens de quelques Theologiens de Hollande, etc.*, which appeared without his name in 1685. The heresy of the pupil much exceeded that of the master. In his sixth letter Le Clerc endeavoured to show that our actual Pentateuch was probably the work of the Israelitish priest, who, after the dissolution of the Northern kingdom, was sent by the King of Assyria from Babylon to instruct the new colonists in the worship of Jehovah; that this priest, either by himself or with assistants, drew up an account of the Creation, and put together extracts from the Israelitish histories and the Mosaic Law-book; and that in this way our Pentateuch originated. Some years afterwards Le Clerc abandoned these wild notions, and in a dissertation prefixed to his commentaries on the Old Testament (1693) ascribed the whole Pentateuch, with the exception of some few later interpolations, to Moses—replying to the doubts and difficulties which he had himself been active in raising. After this time, the question lay at rest for the greater part of the eighteenth century. The high reputation of Carpzovius's learned introduction to the Old Testament, in which the received view of the Pentateuch was strenuously maintained, contributed to silence questionings on the subject in Germany. In Holland the learned were now chiefly engaged with classical and oriental philology. Of English divines, Hody and Kennicott had employed themselves on the original texts of the Old Testament; Lowth, and Blayney, and Newcome were busy with the prophets: and among the Dissenters, Lardner and Benson were exclusively occupied with the New Testament and the evidences of Christianity; and Taylor, whose exact Hebrew scholarship would have well qualified him for the critical investigation of the subject, never ventured to question the traditional theory of the Pentateuch. Far into the latter half of the last century no serious doubts appear to have generally pervaded the theological mind of Europe. Michaelis and Eichhorn, the highest authorities, affirmed to the last the antiquity and substantial authenticity of the Five Books of Moses.

About the middle of the last century a work appeared at Paris, which, though immediately applicable to Genesis alone, exerted a great influence on the subsequent criticism of the entire Pentateuch and of Joshua. Astruc, a French physician, had shown by a careful analysis of Genesis, that Moses, whom he still supposed to be the author of the work, had made use of different documents in constructing it, which might be clearly traced by certain discriminative marks adhering to them through all their combinations. Eichhorn adopted this view, without its at all affecting his belief that Moses was the author of the Pentateuch. Several German scholars, at the end of the last and the commencement of the present century, gave to this discovery of Astruc's a wider application, extended it beyond Genesis into the following books, and began to doubt the Mosaic origin of, at least, the greater part of the Pentateuch. De Wette, in his *Contributions to the Introduction to the Old Testament*, published at Jena, in 1806 and 7, when he was a very young man, with a commendatary preface by Griesbach, carried these new views, which had long been fermenting in the minds of the learned, with extreme fearlessness to their farthest extent. He supposed that the Pentateuch consisted of different parts, which had been written down independently of each other, and that none of these was older than the time of David; that its latest addition was Deuteronomy, which he ascribed to the time of Josiah; and that the Pentateuch, as a whole, did not receive its final form till somewhat later still. The history contained in the Pentateuch, he regarded as unreliable, and its primitive legislation he supposed to have been transmitted from an earlier age through oral tradition.

These bold views De Wette qualified to some extent in the latter years of his life; but they left behind them a deep and uneffaceable effect on the ensuing criticism of the Pentateuch. Meanwhile, the orthodox view was firmly upheld by Jahn, Rosenmüller, and Hug, and in England by Graves and Horne; and to the present day, it still finds zealous and learned representatives abroad in Hengstenberg and Hävernick. Nevertheless, among those who are unbiassed by dogmatic considerations, and bring learning and criticism to the solution of the problem,—there is a remarkable unanimity as to certain general results which they conceive to be established beyond all reasonable doubt, though they differ very considerably from each other in the detail of applying them. De Wette, Stähelin, and Lengerke, Tuch, Ewald, Bertheau, and Bleek, are all obliged to admit, from the unanswerable evidence of internal structure, that the Pentateuch is a very composite work, consisting of materials of different age and authorship, and put into the form in which we now have it at a comparatively recent date, towards the end of the monarchy, perhaps not before the Exile. On all these points they substantially agree; they are at variance with each other—as to the number of the primary documents which have been here combined, their mutual relation, their respective age and probable authorship, and as to the amount of genuine Mosaic elements, whether originally written down, or only transmitted by tradition, which have been preserved in the so-called books of Moses. Even the late Baron Bunsen, in his *Bibelwerk*, while he earnestly clings to the authenticity of the Pentateuch, acknowledges that there is evidence of two distinct periods of legislation, marked by a different character, within the limits of the life of Moses himself, the first more purely ethical, embodied in the Ten Commandments at Sinai, the other descending into legal and ritual enactments in the Transjordanic district, not long before his death; and that around this nucleus, essentially Mosaic, accretions continually gathered at Shiloh, and during the whole time of the Judges and the Kings—the progressive accumulation not ceasing till the reign of Hezekiah, about 700 B.C.—Bleek and Bertheau are decidedly conservative in their theological tendencies, and would properly be classed with the moderate Evangelical school.* To the list of those who have occupied themselves with this question, must be added the name of Dr. Davidson, who, in the first volume of his Introduction to the Old Testament, now in course of publication, has gone into it with a freedom and copiousness of research as yet unsurpassed by any English theologian. To his pages the

* See Bleek's posthumous work, *Einleitung ins A. T.*, from which some of the materials for the preceding history of the controversy have been taken.

English reader is referred for ample information about details which are nowhere else to be found.

In conclusion, it will perhaps be asked, what is the advantage of inquiries like these? Would it not be the wiser course to abstain from unsettling the public mind by raising them? The proper answer is, that solid, healthy instruction can only be based on truth; and that if such inquiries honestly conducted lead to truth, to distrust them is to distrust the God of Truth. If the Father of our Spirits has led us on step by step to the truth, through the inspirations and experiences of Hebrew prophets, let us gratefully and reverentially acknowledge the fact, without presumptuously cavilling about the way in which He has seen fit to bring it to pass. The *modus operandi* belongs to Him, not to us. A clearer insight into the actual composition of the Bible, and a consequent dispersion of the mischievous error of a mechanical, verbal inspiration, will help to extinguish for ever those fruitless controversies which have split up the Christian world into incurable feuds by inflating every little sect with the fond conceit that it could claim for its own particular dogmas the warrant of Divine authority. When the excitement of early prejudice has subsided, it will be seen, that the critical inquiries which search into the primary elements, the constructive laws, and the manifold combinations of a literary composition, must assist the understanding, and draw out the latent significance and beauty of the Bible, as of every other ancient book. Honestly pursued into their natural consequences, they must exalt rather than deaden the devotional sentiment of the reader, by transferring his reverence from "the letter that killeth" to the "spirit which maketh alive."

# ON THE PENTATEUCH,

AND ITS RELATION TO

## THE JEWISH AND CHRISTIAN DISPENSATIONS.

### SECTION I.

PRELIMINARY REMARKS.

Such is the connection between Christianity and the Jewish religion, that the divine origin of the former implies the divine origin of the latter. Christianity, if I may so speak, has made itself responsible for the fact, that the Jewish religion, like itself, proceeded immediately from God. But Christianity has not made itself responsible for the genuineness, the authenticity, or the moral and religious teachings, of that collection of books by Jewish writers, which constitutes the Old Testament. Taken collectively, it may appear, on the one hand, that those books possess a high and very peculiar character, which affords strong evidence of the divine origin of the Jewish religion; and it may appear, on the other hand, that they also contain much that is incredible, and much that does not approve itself to our understanding and moral feelings. But if the latter be the case, it is a fact with which Christianity is not concerned. Our religion is no more answerable for the genuineness, or the contents, of a series of Jewish writings, dating from an uncertain period, and continued till after the return of a part of the nation from the Babylonish captivity, than it is responsible for the genuineness and contents of the works ascribed to Christian authors from the second century to the eleventh. The truth of our religion is no more involved in the truth of all that is related in the Books of Judges, of Kings, and of Chronicles, or in the Pentateuch, supposing the Pentateuch not to be the work of Moses, than it is in the truth of all that is related in the Ecclesiastical Histories of Eusebius, Sozomen, and Theodoret.

If these propositions be true, they go far to remove those difficulties, which not only embarrassed the early Christians, but which have continued to embarrass Christians in every age. But if they be true, a great error has been committed both by Christians and by unbelievers. The most popular and effective objections of unbelievers have been directed not against Christianity, but against the Old Testament, on the ground that Christianity is responsible for the truth, and for the moral and religious character, of all its contents; and, instead of repelling so untenable a proposition, believers have likewise assumed it; or rather they have earnestly affirmed its correctness, and proceeded to argue upon it as they could.

Thus the books composing the Old Testament have been stripped of their true character, which renders them an object of the greatest curiosity and interest; and a false character has been ascribed to them, which brings them into perpetual collision with the moral and religious conceptions of men of more enlightened times than those of their writers, with the principles of rational criticism in the interpretation of language, and even with the progress of the physical sciences. Insuperable objections to the character ascribed to them, objections such as presented themselves to the minds of the early catholic Christians and the Gnostics, lie spread over the surface of these writings. To those objections, thus obvious, familiarity may render us insensible or indifferent. We may pass over them without regard. We may rest in the notion that they admit of some explanation. We may acquiesce, with more or less distrust, in theories and expositions, by which it has been attempted to gloss them over. But, in proportion as these books are critically examined, and as knowledge and correct modes of thinking advance, new objections start up. These, from their novelty, often receive a disproportioned share of notice; and much is thought to be done, if the force of some one that has recently become an object of attention can be broken; while difficulties more important are comparatively neglected.

Everyone knows for how long a time there was a struggle between the authority. falsely ascribed to the Old Testament, and the true system of the planetary motions. It is only within the present century that it may be considered as having ceased, so far as the Roman Catholic church—that is, so far as the majority of Christians—is concerned. In our day the discoveries in geology have, in like manner, been encountered by the narrative given in Genesis of the Creation. Attempts, which to many seem abortive, have been made to reconcile them to each other. But, in the mean time, a greater difficulty, as implying greater ignorance of the true constitution of the physical world, has attracted comparatively little notice, though it occurs likewise in the account of the Creation. It is there taught, according to the obvious meaning of language, that the blue vault of heaven is a solid firmament, separating the waters which are above it from the waters on the earth, and that in this firmament the heavenly bodies are placed.*

The supposed necessity of maintaining the truth of all that the writers of the Old Testament have said or implied has operated, as might be expected, in a manner the most prejudicial to a firm and rational faith in Christianity. The philosopher, who cannot but regard many of the representations of the Deity in the Old Testament as inconsistent with

---

\* "And God made the firmament, and divided the waters which were under the firmament from the waters which were above the firmament : and it was so. And God called the firmament heaven. . . . . And God said, Let there be lights in the firmament of the heaven. . . . . And God set them in the firmament of the heaven to give light on the earth."—Genesis i. 8, 14, 17. Compare the account of the Deluge, in which it is said, that "the windows of heaven were opened ; " and Psalm cxlviii. 4, where "the waters above the heavens" are called upon to praise the Lord.

his character; the enlightened Christian, who is unable to believe that God commanded the indiscriminate massacre of men, women, and children, by his chosen people, in order to prepare them for his service; the moralist, who perceives that the principles and feelings, expressed or approved in portions of these books, belong to an unenlightened and barbarous age; the careful inquirer, who finds that there are parts of the history which he cannot receive as true, because they involve contradictions, or are contrary to all probability,—he, in a word, who, examining without prejudice, sees the many objections to which the Old Testament is exposed, when put forward as an authoritative guide in religion, morals, and history, (even if such authority be not claimed for it in the physical sciences,)—is told that, if he would be a Christian, he must renounce his objections, and that it is a part of his religion to receive the Old Testament as bearing such a character. The solutions of the objections to its supposed character, which have been offered by wise and good men, are often such that it is difficult to believe them to have been satisfactory to the proposer. They proceed on false principles, or assume facts without foundation. They are often superficial, evasive, or incoherent. They appear to result from a feeling of the necessity of saying something. They are often such as can be regarded by any one as admissible only on the ground, that there must be some mode of explaining away all such objections, and, therefore, that there is, in every case, a presumption in favour of a particular explanation, when no other can be found so plausible. Thus, then, the truth of Christianity having been made to appear as implicated in the truth of a position that cannot be maintained, its evidences, though their intrinsic validity has not been weakened, have been deprived of much of their power over the minds of men.

In expressing these opinions, one is but giving form and voice to the ideas and feelings that exist in the minds of a large portion of intelligent believers. There is nothing in them of novelty or boldness. One is but saying what many have thought before him with more or less distinctness.

for mentioning that the substance of what follows was originally committed to writing more than ten years ago (in the summer of 1831), and that I have not since found occasion to make any essential change in my conclusions.

## SECTION II.

### ON THE EVIDENCES AND THE DESIGN OF THE JEWISH DISPENSATION.

THE belief that Moses was an inspired messenger of God follows from our belief in the divine origin of Christianity. He was, we suppose, miraculously commissioned to give to the Jews a knowledge of God, as the Maker and Governor of all things, and such other just conceptions of Him as they were capable of receiving; and to teach them to regard themselves as having been separated from the rest of men, by having been called in a peculiar manner to worship and serve Him. Beside the attestation to the divine origin of the Jewish dispensation furnished by Christianity, there are independent proofs of it, to which, without dwelling upon them at length, it may be worth while to advert.

When we consider what the Jews were in other respects, the simple, direct knowledge which they possessed of God, as the sole Maker and Governor of the Universe, presenting so striking a contrast to the mythology of the most enlightened portion of the ancient world, affords the strongest confirmation of what they asserted, that its source was a divine revelation. This appears more clearly, when we reflect, that the idea of God was not with them a matter of speculation among a few philosophers, but formed the fundamental doctrine of their popular faith. The mere fact, likewise, of their most extraordinary belief, that they had been separated from all other nations, by being called to worship Him, admits, apparently, of no other solution than that their belief was true. The high and just representations of the Deity, the exalted language of piety, and the noble and enlightened views of duty, which we find in the Scriptures of the Jews, when compared with what appears in other portions of those Scriptures, with the prevailing character of the Jews themselves, and with that of other ancient nations, can, as far as we are able to discern, be referred only to the deep influences of a divine revelation upon their minds. We perceive these influences in the formation of poetical writings of a kind to which nothing similar can be produced. They are compositions of the most marked religious character, altogether unlike the poetry of other ancient nations. The individuals addressed are throughout regarded under one aspect, as distinguished from all other men by the peculiar relation in which they stood towards God. In the more eminent of these works, in those, for example, which have been ascribed to Isaiah, we perceive, that the powerful mind, the strong feelings, and splendid imagination of the writer, had been thoroughly wrought upon by religious convictions, which we cannot reasonably ascribe to the unaided progress of the human intellect among the Jews. Looking to the time when that people were already in possession of those wonderful books, we have to cast our view back to a period lighted only by a few gleams of authentic history. Here, we see men collecting in groups to listen to the poems of Homer, in which the objects of their worship are pictured with the vices and passions of the gross and ferocious chieftains of the age; there, we behold the gigantic monuments which Egyptian superstition had raised to its monster gods; all around is the darkness and error of polytheism, in one form or other, except where a small people rise distinctly to view, separate from the rest of mankind; a people of which there are now no famous monuments, but its own continued existence and its sacred writings. Among the Jews, long before Socrates would have taught the Athenians the goodness and providence of the *gods*, there was a familiar conception of God; and their prophets could thus address them:—

"Have ye not known? Have ye not heard? Jehovah is

the eternal God, the creator of the ends of the earth. He faints not, neither is weary. There is no searching of his understanding."

"Thus says Jehovah, the king of Israel, I am the first, and I am the last, and beside me there is no God."

"Let the wicked man forsake his way, and the unrighteous man his thoughts, and let him return to Jehovah, and he will have mercy upon him, and to our God, for he will abundantly pardon.

"For your thoughts are not my thoughts, nor your ways my ways, says Jehovah.

"For as the heavens are higher than the earth, so are my ways higher than your ways, and my thoughts than your thoughts."

They who habitually expressed these and corresponding conceptions of the Supreme Being, believed that they had derived them from express revelation; and there appears no good reason for doubting the correctness of their belief.

But it is not merely in the more remarkable portions of Hebrew poetry, that we find conceptions which we can account for only by referring them to a divine revelation. The Jews have left us a large collection of books, most of them in existence five centuries before Christ, throughout which, with the exception of two (the Song of Solomon, so called, and the Book of Esther), there runs a constant recognition of the being, providence, and moral government of God. The Old Testament, so insulated from all other productions of the human mind in ancient times, presents a great phenomenon in the intellectual history of our race. We may explain it at once, if we admit the divine origin of the Jewish religion; and what other solution but this can be offered?

There is another striking consideration. We can discern nothing but the fact, that the religion of the Jews had been confirmed to them by indisputable evidence, as a revelation from God, which could have wrought in their minds such an invincible conviction of its truth, as to have preserved them a distinct people from a period beyond any connected and authentic records of profane history to the present day. In maintaining their faith they were for more than twenty centuries exposing themselves to the outrages of Heathens and Christians;—to a persecution which even now has not everywhere subsided. Driven from their native soil, scattered among enemies, insulted, trampled upon, cruelly wronged, they have still clung to their religion, the cause of their sufferings, with inveterate constancy. From an antiquity which would be shrouded in darkness, were not a dim light cast upon it by their own history, this small people has flowed down an unmingled stream amid the stormy waves of the world. For a phenomenon so marvellous it is idle to assign any ordinary causes. One cause alone explains it. We must regard it as an inexplicable wonder, or we must believe, that this people were, as they profess, separated from the rest of men by God, and this in a manner so evident, solemn, and effectual, that the ineffaceable belief of the fact has been transmitted from generation to generation, as an essential characteristic of the race.

Thus we perceive, that, beside the attestation of Christianity to its truth, the Jewish dispensation has independent evidence of its own; evidence, which, so intimate is the connection between them, is reflected on Christianity itself.

If it be asked, what was the design of the Jewish dispensation? the answer seems to be, that its main, I do not say its sole, purpose was to serve as a groundwork for Christianity. Supposing that no nation like the Jews had existed, and that polytheism had prevailed throughout the world, a messenger from God, such as Jesus Christ, must have had no small difficulty to encounter on the very threshold of his ministry in making his character and office understood by men ignorant of God. If he had appeared, for instance, at Athens or Rome, the very annunciation of his claims to authority would have been a sudden and strange attack on the whole established system of religion. A new and vast conception, that of God, must have been formed in the

But he, who discusses the errors that have been connected with our religion, for the purpose of separating them from it, and preventing their further hindrance to its reception and influence, must prosecute his labour under a great disadvantage; for he is liable to be altogether misunderstood or misrepresented. There are two classes of writers, who, with wholly opposite views, have called attention to these errors. One class consists of those who have confounded them with our religion, who regard them as essential parts of it, who direct their reasoning or their ridicule against them, and, in exposing them, consider themselves as confuting the claims of Christianity. The other class is composed of such as, with a deep sense of the value of our religion, are solicitous to remove from it all that has obscured its character and weakened its power. The purpose of one class is the very opposite of that of the other; but they agree as to the nature of the errors. By both they are equally considered as indefensible; and often this correspondence alone is regarded; and the most earnest defenders of Christianity have been confounded with its enemies, by such Christians as agree with its enemies in viewing those errors as essential to our faith.

It is, at the same time, not to be doubted, that he, who has been compelled to renounce many prejudices respecting Christianity is in danger of becoming unable to discriminate between what is true and what is false, and, consequently, of renouncing our religion altogether. As he relinquishes one doctrine after another, which he had held as a part of his faith, a sceptical turn of mind is likely to be formed; a prejudice may grow up against whatever has been received as true; his judgment may become bewildered, and he may lose confidence in its decisions, except when they favour unbelief; while, having been led wrong by the guides whom he had trusted, he is also deprived of that reliance on the judgment of others, which is so often important or necessary to the strength of our convictions, and even to the formation of our opinions. All this may take place in the mind of one whose intentions and feelings are wholly honest. Religious truth, which so many have been seeking for so many centuries, and which, amid the vast diversity and opposition of opinions, it is clear that so few can have found, is not to be secured by mere honesty of intention and feeling. To separate from Christianity what has been erroneously connected with it, and what has become incorporated with the religion of many Christians—I mean, to effect the separation in one's own mind—is not an easy task. It is not strange that some, whose attention has been strongly directed to those errors, should have failed to accomplish it; that they should have wanted the learning and judgment, the power of discrimination, the integrity of purpose, the just conception of the essential character of Christianity, and the deep sense of its value, which are prerequisites and sufficient safeguards in the inquiry; and that, having begun as reformers, they should have ended in being unbelievers.

Equally by those who consecrate the errors of Christians as parts of Christianity, and by those who reject our religion on account of them, a rational Christian is liable to be questioned, how it is that he retains his Christian faith, while he puts aside so much that Christians have believed; and it may be suggested to him by both parties, that, if he will but follow out his principles, he will become an infidel. But the gross errors which a great majority of Christians have fallen into, tend in no degree to invalidate the evidences of Christianity. The inquiry concerning those errors has no bearing on the intrinsic weight of its evidences. That the professed disciples of Christ, through eighteen centuries, have not been miraculously divested of the infirmities and vices of their fellow-men, and thus secured from religious error, is a fact, which, however striking or shocking are the illustrations that may be given of it, cannot be brought to disprove the proposition, that Christ was a teacher from God. It does not follow that there is no truth, or that there is no evidence sufficient to establish the truth, concerning the highest objects of human thought, because a very great majority of our race has fallen into essential mistakes concerning them. Christianity may be true, notwithstanding the false doctrines that have accumulated round it; just as it is true, that the heavenly bodies exist and move, notwithstanding the prevailing theories concerning them from the beginning of science to the sixteenth century were wholly erroneous.

It is evident from what has been said, that he who is about to direct his attention to the errors which men have fallen into respecting religion, should settle in his mind what religion is, and what Christianity is, and in what their value consists. It may be said, that this should be a result of the inquiry, not a preliminary to it; that we must first ascertain how far Christians have been in error, before we can determine what is to be received as true. But such is not the case. Reasoning philosophically, we are not first to inquire into what men have believed, whether correctly or not; we are to look only at the essential considerations which should determine our judgment concerning religion and Christianity.

All religion is founded solely on two facts, the existence of God, and the immortality of man. Our relations to the Infinite Spirit and to the endless future alone constitute us religious beings. If we knew, that there was no God and Father of the Universe, and that we were to perish when we die, there could be no religion. It is through faith in God and immortality, that man ceases to appear as a blind, suffering, short-lived creature of earth, and becomes transformed into a being, capable of the noblest views and aspirations, of unlimited progress in virtue and happiness; having a permanent tenure in the Universe, the eternal care of God.

Religion must not be confounded with superstition. The belief of error is not the same thing as the belief of truth. The imperfection of language has in this, as in a thousand other cases, led to a great mistake; for in one sense of the word *religion*, we apply it to the superstitions, or false religions, that have existed in the world; and men have, in consequence, classed them together with true religion, as if they all possessed a character essentially alike. But true religion and false religion are essentially different.

It has been vaguely and erroneously said, that all men, whether enlightened by revelation or not, have a belief in God; and this belief has been represented as instinctive, or intuitive, as a matter of consciousness, as a part of our nature, or as necessarily resulting from our nature. The proposition has no other foundation than this, that all men are compelled to recognize the fact, that there are powers, that is, agencies, without them, stronger than they, by which their actions are controlled, and their condition essentially affected. To these powers, by an act of imagination and association, similar to that which leads a child to love the inanimate object that pleases it, or to be angry with that which hurts it, men have transferred moral qualities, and thus personified them; they have endued inanimate objects, with life and worshipped them, as the sun, moon, and stars, or they have ascribed the effects experienced to some imaginary being, or to some being whose power had been felt on earth. But the obvious recognition of an indisputable fact, accompanied by one of the most ordinary operations of the mind, is not religion. It does not constitute faith in God. The believer in the Egyptian mythology, or in the fabulous gods of Greece and Rome, was not a believer in God. There was nothing in his opinions or imaginations to produce those sentiments, or that character, which are the proper result of a Christian's faith. The heathen gods were but rulers of the same essential nature with earthly despots. The belief in them was not elevating but degrading. The heathen religions consecrated vice in their very solemnities, but offered no encouragements to virtue, and no consolations or hopes to suffering man. The Jewish and Christian Scriptures truly represent idolatry, not as it has been conceived of in modern times, as an imperfect developement of true religion, but as its opposite.

There is no instinctive, intuitive, or direct knowledge of the truths of religion; neither of the being of God, nor of our own immortality. It is scarcely a matter of dispute, if indeed it be at all a matter of dispute, that of our own immortality,—the great fact which changes the aspect of all things and assimilates man to the Divinity; the fact, without the belief, or, at least, without the hope of which, there can be no religion,—that of our own immortality we can be assured only by revelation. It may indeed be the case, that a being of perfect reason might, from the phenomena of the present state known to man, infer not only the existence of God, but our power of attaining an immortal existence. But man is not a being of perfect reason; and of the individuals who compose our race there are comparatively very few who have a wide acquaintance with the phenomena of the present state, or who are capable of reasoning on any subject remote from their common experience. It is not necessary, however, to inquire, as if the question were unsettled, what the collective wisdom of men, unassisted by revelation, can effect toward producing a conviction of the essential truths of religion. The question has been answered. It is answered in the teachings of Socrates, and in the writings of Plato, Aristotle, and Cicero. They had no distinct conception of God, as God is conceived of by an enlightened Christian. They had either no belief, or no confident belief, of the personal immortality of individual men. If any one doubt these statements, they require explanation and discussion. But there is something more to be said. The question is further answered—and this answer requires no explanation, for it admits of no controversy—by the state of religion among their contemporaries, by the general absence of any conception of God, or of any assurance of immortality. It is answered in the mythology of the Hindoos, in the adoration of human divinities by the Buddhists, degenerating into the worship of the Dalai-lama, and in the other superstitions which, in ancient and modern times, have overspread the earth where the light of revelation has not shone.

Undoubtedly, there are very noble conceptions of the

Divinity, mixed, however, with much that is altogether incongruous, in the speculations of ancient sages. Such conceptions appear, for example, in the writings of Plato, and in the Vedas and other sacred books of the Hindoos. But the question is not, what a few philosophers, unenlightened by revelation, have believed or imagined, but what the generality of men, unenlightened by revelation, have believed or imagined. However strong the evidence of religious truth from the phenomena of nature may be in the abstract, and very strong undoubtedly it is, yet the fact is proved by the experience of the world, it is proved, I believe, by the personal experience of everyone who has thought and felt deeply on the subject, that men, left to themselves, are incapable of grasping and estimating it, and of resting satisfied in the conclusions to which it leads,—conclusions, so remote from the interests and passions of this world, so beyond the sphere of our ordinary experience, and sometimes so apparently contradictory to it. Who, not instructed by revelation, can look on death, and feel assured of immortality? Upon this evidence alone religion has never been established among men. This alone has never solved the difficulties nor quieted the doubts of one anxious and philosophical inquirer. It has never defined the idea of God, as God is revealed by Christianity. It has never afforded any one a conviction of his being formed for eternal progress in improvement and happiness.

Our belief in God, then, as the Father of men, and our belief in our own immortality, truths, which may well seem to be too vast for human comprehension, if we were left to our unassisted powers, rest on our belief, that their evidence is the testimony of God through the mission and teachings of Jesus Christ. I say his mission;—for his mission from God to men, if that fact be established, is alone a virtual revelation of the essential truths of religion. In this age of scepticism and false philosophy, it may be said, that such a communication from God to men is hard to be conceived of or believed. Be it so, but let it be remembered, that on the decision of the question, whether such a communication have been made or not, depends the existence of religion among men;—I do not say of superstition; that flourishes rankly when its growth is not overshadowed and kept down by religion; and still less do I speak of the temporary existence of religious mysticism, which is but another word for feelings, the result of education and habit, for which no reason can be given. Religion is either identified with Christianity, or subsists in those who reject Christianity, through its still remaining power; as an evergreen severed from its root may for a time retain the appearance of life.

The fundamental truths of religion, as taught by Christianity, necessarily imply the fact, or, in other words, involve the truth, that we shall always be subject to the moral government of God; to that government which connects happiness with the observance of those laws that are essential to the nature of every moral being, and suffering with their transgression. Under this aspect the practical bearing of religion appears. Thus, when assured of the truths which it teaches, we know all that is necessary for our virtue and happiness. We know what may inspire the most glorious hopes, what may animate us in every effort for our own improvement and the service of our fellow-creatures; we know all that we need to strengthen us for the endless course that lies before us.

With these truths settled in our minds, we may enter without anxiety on the examination of the many and opposite opinions, true and false, which different parties among Christians have connected with their faith in Christianity. In rejecting far the larger number of them as unfounded, an enlightened and well-informed man will perceive that he is merely arriving at conclusions, to which the progress of the human mind in knowledge and in correct modes of thinking has been gradually conducting us; and that this progress, while it has undermined those errors, has tended equally to confirm the evidence of the essential principles of religion. He will do honour to his predecessors, who, without discerning all the truth, toiled and suffered in opening the way to it. He will not regard himself as superior to those, through whose labours his intellect has been formed, because through their assistance he has advanced somewhat further than they had done. He will not fancy that in the present age there has been a great outbreak of wisdom, from some hitherto unknown source, which is to sweep away all that has been established and revered. Nor in his mind will pernicious errors and essential truths be so bound together by his prejudices that he cannot free himself from the former without loosening the latter from their hold.

Far from it. Every truth concerning our religion and its evidences is connected with and confirms every other; and in removing an error we are establishing a truth. Then only may we hope that the evidences of Christianity will be allowed their full weight, and the efficacy of its doctrines be obstructed only by the imperfections and passions essential to our nature, when it shall be presented as it is, separate from all the erroneous opinions and false doctrines that have been connected with it. As one truth confirms another, so one error gives birth to another, often producing a numerous brood; and the system into which any important error enters, as an essential part, becomes either corrupted throughout, or inconsistent with itself.

These observations will not be regarded as out of place, when it is perceived that the inquiry on which we are about to enter leads to conclusions, different from the opinions which have been professed by the generality of Christians; though, unquestionably, the considerations on which those conclusions are founded have presented themselves to the minds of a great portion of intelligent believers.

I will venture to add a word or two more, having somewhat of a personal bearing. It seems to me a weighty offence against society, to advance and maintain opinions on any important subject, especially any subject connected with religion, without carefully weighing them, and without feeling assured, as far as may be, that we shall find no reason to change our belief. I may be excused, therefore, minds of men before they could have a notion of the peculiar office of him who addressed them. When we look at the state of either city, it seems scarcely possible that he should have been able to collect an audience, except of such as might have flocked to him as an extraordinary magician or theurgist. If we imagine him to have been listened to by some with deference, as a religious teacher, yet how large a portion of such hearers would have confounded the idea of the Supreme Being, *to whom there is nothing similar or second*, with that of Jupiter, to whom, in a very limited sense, and in the language of poetical flattery, they had been accustomed to apply such expressions; and how many might have mistaken the messenger himself for *Mercury, or some other god, come down in the likeness of a man.*\* There would have been no preparation for his advent, no expectation of it, no previous conception of its nature. It would have been an insulated, incomprehensible event, connected with nothing in their history or their former belief. The ground would not have been cleared for exhibiting before mankind the marvellous transactions of such a ministry as that of Christ.

This view of the important purpose of the Jewish dispensation may further tend to assure us of its divine origin. But to maintain that Moses was a minister of God is one thing, and to maintain that he was the author of the Pentateuch is another. So far is the truth of either proposition from being involved in that of the other, that in order to render it evident that Moses was from God, it may be necessary to prove that the books which profess to contain a history of his ministry were not written by him, and do not afford an authentic account of it. Whether this be so or not, may appear in some degree from what follows, in which I shall examine the probability of the supposition that these books were written by Moses.

\* Acts xiv. 11, 12.

# SECTION III.

## ON THE HISTORICAL EVIDENCE RESPECTING THE AUTHORSHIP OF THE PENTATEUCH.

In determining whether an ancient work is to be ascribed to a particular author, we must begin with the historical evidence.

Respecting the Pentateuch we will first consider *the evidence that relates to its history subsequent to the return of the Jews from their Captivity* (B.C. 536). This evidence is sufficient to render it probable that it was in existence somewhere about a century after that event. The date that has been assigned for Ezra's reading "the Law of Moses" to the people, as related in the eighth chapter of Nehemiah, is the year 454 before Christ.* "Ezra," says Prideaux, "reformed the whole state of the Jewish Church according to the Law of Moses, in which he was excellently learned, and settled it upon that bottom, upon which it afterwards stood to the time of our Saviour."† This statement expresses what has been the common belief on the subject. Perhaps too much agency may be ascribed in it to Ezra alone. But it seems not improbable that within his lifetime the Jews, who had returned to Palestine, were formed anew into a State, on the basis, generally, of the Levitical Law. Ezra, it is said, read the book of the Law of Moses to the people. But there is nothing to identify this Book of the Law with the whole five books of the Pentateuch. Admitting that the Levitical Law existed in all its extent in the time of Ezra, yet we cannot infer from this fact alone that it was then incorporated with the historical portion of the Pentateuch. If this union, however, did not then exist, it was probably effected not long after. The Septuagint translation of the

---

* That is, about a thousand years, as commonly reckoned, after the death of Moses, B.C. 1451. [Bunsen, in his Biblische Jahrbücher (Bibelwerk, I.), places the death of Moses 1300 B.C. ; but this variation does not affect the general argument.—ED.]

† Prideaux's Connection of the History of the Old and New Testament, Part i. Book 5. Vol. ii. p. 460. 10th Ed. 1729.

Pentateuch was made in the first half of the third century before Christ. The origin of the Samaritan Pentateuch (that which was used by the Samaritans, written in their own alphabetical characters), we may, with Prideaux and others,* refer to the time when a temple was built on Mount Gerizim, and the temple-worship introduced among the Samaritans by Manasseh and his associates, as related by Josephus. This, according to Josephus,† was during the reign of Alexander, about 330 years before Christ. Some, however, have assigned to it an earlier date—namely, about the beginning of the fourth century before Christ.‡

But, if the Pentateuch existed in the time of Ezra, or not long after, this fact alone does not afford any proof that it was then ascribed to Moses as its author. To this point we shall hereafter advert. But we may here observe that the Pentateuch itself, while it assumes to be an authentic account of the deeds and laws of Moses, puts forward no claim to being considered as his work. Though he were not regarded as its author in the time of Ezra, it might be readily received by the Jews as bearing the character of an authentic document.

The fact that "the Law" was ascribed to Moses does not prove that the authorship of the Pentateuch was ascribed to him. But that he was generally regarded by the Jews as its author, about the commencement of our era, appears from Philo, the writers of the New Testament, and Josephus. The prevalence of this opinion at that time shows that it was not of recent origin; but affords no ground for determining its antiquity within any precise limits.

We have no further knowledge of the history of the Pentateuch between the time of the return of the Jews to Pales-

* Prideaux's Connection, Part i. Book 6. Vol. ii. p. 597, seqq.—Simon, Histoire Crit. du V. T. Liv. i. c. 10.—Idem, Critique de la Bibliothèque et des Prolégomènes de M. du Pin. Tome iii. p. 148, seqq.—Van Dale, De Origine et Progressu Idolatriæ, pp. 75-82. p. 681, seqq.—Gesenius, De Pentateucho Samaritano, § 2.

† Antiq. Jud. Lib. xi. ch. 7, 8.

‡ Compare Josephus with Nehemiah, xiii. 28, and see Prideaux's Connection, P. i. B. 6. Vol. ii. p. 588, seqq.

tine and the commencement of the Christian era, an interval of more than five centuries, except that it was included in the class of books which at the last-mentioned date we find considered by the Jews as sacred books, or, in other words, included in the "Canon," as it is called, of the Old Testament. Respecting this canon there are also some traditions of the Jews which deserve notice. We will next attend, therefore, to its history, and to these traditions.

From an age considerably before the time of Josephus, as is evident from a passage in that writer, and from other considerations on which our subject does not require us to dwell, the books *now regarded by Protestants* as forming the Old Testament,* have been recognized by the Jews as sacred books. But this canon was not formed, or, in other words, it was not settled what books should be classed together as possessing in some respects a common, I do not say a sacred, character, till after the return of the Jews to Palestine. This is evident from the fact of its containing books, about which there is no controversy, that they were not written till after that event—namely, the Chronicles, the books of Ezra and Nehemiah, and those of Haggai, Zechariah, and Malachi. Of the history of the formation of the canon we are wholly ignorant. In the reign of Josiah, a little before the commencement of the Captivity, it appears, from a narrative in the Book of Kings, that the Jews generally were ignorant of the existence of a written copy of their national laws, before the discovery, as represented, of such a copy in the Temple.† On their return it is probable that a large majority of them, taken individually, were not acquainted with all those writings of the Old Testament which were then extant. Some,

---

\* To these the Council of Trent (A.D. 1546) added, as of equal authority, all those books, and parts of books, which constitute the Apocrypha of our English Bibles, except the two books of Esdras (Ezra), so called, and the prayer of Manasseh. It is not here the place to give an account of the manner in which the more intelligent Roman Catholics explain, or evade, this decree of the last General Council,—the last which will ever be held.

† 2 Kings xxii.

perhaps, knew of one work and some of another. Such being the case, we have no credible information respecting the manner in which these books, together with the others afterwards classed with them, were brought into notice, and finally came to be considered as the sacred books of the nation. But though we have no direct evidence on this subject, we have, perhaps, ground for a probable conjecture. These books are very diverse in their character. The contents of many of them, as, for example, Ruth, the Proverbs, Ecclesiastes, the Song of Solomon, Ezra, and Nehemiah (to mention no others), are such as not to afford any very obvious reason or occasion for ascribing to them a sacred character. The admission of these books into the canon is to be viewed in connection with the fact, that no ancient Hebrew work not included in it is known to have existed at the time when the canon may be supposed to have been completed. Hence we may infer that this class of books was formed upon *no principle of selection.* It is probable that it comprehended *all* the remains of the ancient literature of the nation; all books—that is to say, all books intended for general use, and of any value or notoriety—which had escaped the ravages of war and the injuries of time. They had all a common character, as, with the exception of the use of the Chaldee language in portions of two of those of latest date, Ezra and Daniel, they were all written in the Hebrew language, a language which had become obsolete. Far the greater portion of them were of the highest national interest, as relating either to the religion and laws of the nation, or to its history, which was so intimately connected with the national religion. Others of a different kind had, or were supposed to have, sufficient claims to be classed with them; as the Proverbs and the Song of Solomon, the latter of which, and many of the former, were ascribed to the most powerful monarch of the nation, the wisest of men. We perceive at once how a sacred character might be assigned to many of these books; and it is easy to understand how such a character should, in process of time, be extended to all.

We are ignorant how far the preservation of these books, and their final reception as sacred writings, were the result of a general estimate of their value, or how much was effected by the care and efforts of some leading individual or individuals. One fact, however, respecting them is evident. Some of them must have been compiled after the composition of the parts, or writings, of which they are respectively formed; as the book of Psalms, the book of Proverbs (which consists of several collections of those ascribed to Solomon, together with those ascribed to Agar, and those, as is said, of the mother of a king Lemuel, who is not elsewhere mentioned\*), and the works of some of the prophets, which consist of separate and unconnected prophecies or poems. In the compilation of the latter works there is little doubt that errors have been committed; and that compositions have been ascribed to some of the prophets, particularly to Isaiah, of which they were not the authors. The book of Nehemiah, likewise, was originally united with that of Ezra, as forming together with it one work, to which the name of the latter was given; and it appears that Ezra was regarded as in some sense the author of both. Each of these two books, moreover, appears to be a compilation, inartificially put together, so as to occasion historical and chronological difficulties. Only a portion of each can be referred to the individual whose name it bears.

It has been commonly said by modern writers, that Ezra, after the return from the Captivity, revised and re-edited the books of the Old Testament; that is, as the proposition must be understood, those books which were extant at the time of his performing this work. The statement rests on a Jewish tradition. But this tradition first appears at much too late a period to be regarded as any evidence of the fact. It, moreover, presents itself in a shape obviously fabulous. It is not mentioned by Philo or Josephus; nor is it found

---

\* See Proverbs i. 1 ; x. 1 ; xxv. 1 ; xxx. 1 ; xxxi. 1.

in the Talmud. There is a passage in what is called the Second Book of Esdras (Ezra), a book of uncertain origin and date, published among the Apocrypha of the English Bible, which appears to be founded on it. In this passage the Law is said to have been burnt, so that no man knew the things that had been done by God; and Ezra is represented as proposing, through the assistance of the Holy Spirit, to write over again what had been written in the Law.* The tradition in question is to be traced principally in the works of the Christian fathers, who undoubtedly derived it from the Jews. The earliest writer by whom it is distinctly mentioned is Irenæus, who lived six centuries after the time of Ezra. He says, that, "the Scriptures having been destroyed" at the time of the Captivity, God "inspired Ezra to put in order all the words of the preceding prophets, and to restore to the people the Law which was given by Moses."† A similar account is found in Clement of Alexandria. The Scriptures being destroyed, he says, Ezra was inspired to renew them, and to make them known again to the people.‡ Tertullian says, that "it is well known that, after the destruction of Jerusalem by the Babylonians, the whole body of the Jewish writings was restored anew by Ezra."§ Chrysostom seems to have been unwilling to admit the marvellous part of the story in its full extent; for, though he speaks of the books of the Jewish Scriptures as having been burnt, he appears not to have been disposed to believe that they were utterly destroyed. God, he says, who had inspired Moses and the prophets, "inspired another admirable man, Ezra, to set them forth, and put them together *from their remains.*"∥ Theodoret, on the one hand, represents the books as having been entirely destroyed, and restored by Ezra, through Divine inspiration.¶ The tradition which appears under

* 2 Esdras xiv. 21, seqq.
† Cont. Hæres. Lib. iii. c. 21, § 2, p. 216.
‡ Stromat. i. § 21, p. 392; § 22, p. 410.
§ De Cultu Feminarum, § 3, p. 151. [De Habitu Muliebri, c. 3.—ED.]
∥ Homil. viii. in Epist. ad Hebræos.
¶ Interpret. in Cant. Cantic. Opp. i. 934, 985.

these forms shows, that the Jews, at the time when they transmitted their ancient books to Christians, were ignorant of the history of them, and had substituted fables for facts.

This is further made evident by a tradition preserved in the Talmud concerning their canonical books.* "Moses," it is there said, "wrote his book, the section concerning Balaam,† and Job. Joshua wrote his book, and eight verses which are in the Law.‡ Samuel wrote his book, the book of Judges and Ruth. David wrote the book of Psalms with the assistance [*per manus*] of ten of the Elders, Adam, Melchisedec, Abraham, Moses, Heman, Jeduthan, Asaph, and the three sons of Korah.§ Jeremiah wrote his book, the book of Kings, and the Lamentations. Hezekiah [the king of Judah], with his ministers, *wrote*‖ the prophecies of Isaiah, the Proverbs, the Canticles, and Ecclesiastes. The men of the Great Synagogue¶ *wrote* Ezekiel,

* Vid. Wolfii Biblioth. Rabbin. Tom. ii. pp. 2, 3.

† "The section concerning Balaam, or of Balaam." These words have been differently understood by the later Jewish commentators. Some suppose, that Moses wrote a separate account of Balaam, apart from the Pentateuch. Others, that the account found in the Pentateuch (Numbers xxii.-xxiv.) was translated by Moses from a book written by Balaam himself. See Fabricii Codex Pseudepig. V. T. Tom. i. pp. 809, 810.

‡ This seems to refer to what is said in Joshua xxiv. 26.

§ The Jews ascribed the ninety-second Psalm to Adam, the hundred and tenth to Melchisedec, the ninetieth to Moses, whose name appears in the inscription to it in our English Bible, and others to the different individuals mentioned, whose names, with the exception of that of Abraham, are likewise found in the present inscriptions in the Psalms.

‖ This word *wrote*, here, and where it is again italicized, appears to be used very loosely, and in different senses, in respect to the different books mentioned. It is to be understood, perhaps, in reference to some of these books, as meaning that the persons spoken of committed to writing what before had been orally preserved ; and, in respect to others, that they brought together the different parts of which the book is formed ; that they compiled it. In reference to the book of Esther, it may mean that they composed it.

The notion, that Hezekiah, with his associates, was engaged in this work, was undoubtedly derived from Proverbs xxv. 1. "These are also proverbs of Solomon, which the men of Hezekiah, king of Judah, copied out."

¶ The Great Synagogue, according to a fiction of the Jewish Rabbins, was a council of one hundred and twenty men, over whom Ezra presided, and who assisted him in the re-establishment of the polity and relation of the nation after the return of the Jews to Palestine. See Buxtorf's Tiberias, cap. x. p. 93, seq.

the twelve Minor Prophets, Daniel, and Esther. Ezra wrote his book* and the Chronicles."

Thus far we have found nothing which bears the character of historical evidence to show that Moses was the author of the Pentateuch. We have found no proof even that such was the opinion of the Jews in the time of Ezra. Nor, indeed, have we found any decisive proof that the Pentateuch was in existence in his time; for we have no good reason for believing that, when the Law of Moses is spoken of, the Pentateuch is necessarily intended. But, could it be proved that the Pentateuch, in the time of Ezra, was believed by the Jews to be the work of Moses, we should still be a thousand years distant from the time of Moses; and an opinion respecting the authorship of a book, existing at a period a thousand years distant from the time of its supposed writer, cannot be regarded as historical evidence.

It is clear, therefore, from the nature of the case, that there exists no historical evidence that Moses was the author of the Pentateuch, unless it may be found in some of the other books which compose the Jewish canon. No other documents make such an approach toward the time of Moses, as may entitle them to any weight in support of the supposition, that he was the author of the Pentateuch. We will, then, next consider *the historical evidence which has been thought to be furnished by the Old Testament itself.*

In the other books of the Old Testament there are references to various narratives and laws now found in the Pentateuch, and these references have been considered as proving that the Pentateuch was in existence before their composition, and consequently as furnishing indirect proof that it was written by Moses. But such references afford no ground for these conclusions; for, if the Pentateuch were not the work of Moses, it was undoubtedly, in great part, a compilation (derived from ancient authorities, written

---

* By "his book, as already mentioned, is meant not only that which passes under the name of Ezra, but likewise that ascribed to Nehemiah.

or oral, or both), which was made for the purpose of embodying and preserving the traditions and national laws of the Jews: and there is no reason why those traditions and laws should not have been referred to as well before its existence as after.

In the Book of Joshua there is repeated mention of "the Book of the Law of Moses;" and hence it has been argued, that we have evidence of the earliest date to justify us in ascribing the Pentateuch to Moses. But such is not the case. We must here, as elsewhere, keep in mind, that there is nothing to identify "the Book of the Law of Moses," or, in other words, a written collection of the laws ascribed to Moses, with the whole Pentateuch, previously to the time when it may be proved, by wholly independent evidence, that those laws were to be found in the last four books of the Pentateuch, and that the whole five had become so connected together as to be designated by the common title of "the Book of the Law." But, though it may be well to keep this consideration in view, yet it is not important in its bearing on the case before us. The main fact to be at present attended to is, that there is no evidence to show, when or by whom the Book of Joshua was written. Its history and age are at least as uncertain as those of the five books ascribed to Moses; and it is so connected with them, and liable to so many common or similar objections, that its authority must stand or fall together with that of the Pentateuch.*

* It is remarkable, that the references in Joshua to a Book of the Law, when taken together, are of such a character, as rather to throw discredit on the work in which they are found, than to serve to confirm the credit of any other. In the first chapter (vv. 7, 8,) Joshua is represented as being enjoined by the Lord "to do according to the Law which Moses commanded," and "to meditate day and night on the Book of the Law." Here, by "the Book of the Law," it may seem that the writer intended either the whole Pentateuch, or the book of Deuteronomy alone. I mention the last supposition, because there seem to be no clear references in Joshua to any book of the Pentateuch except Deuteronomy. If, however, this book alone were referred to as the Book of the Law, it would prove the writer's ignorance or disregard of the four other books of the Pentateuch, and afford proof, that in his day they were either not in existence, or not attributed to Moses. It may be assumed, therefore, that the whole Pentateuch is meant. In the last chapter (v. 26) it is

In the seventh verse of the fortieth Psalm, ascribed to David, there is mention of a book, which has been supposed to be the Pentateuch. The verse is thus given in the Common Version.

said, that Joshua wrote "these words" (it is not clear what words. are intended) in "the Book of the Law of God." Here again it may seem that some copy either of Deuteronomy or of the whole Pentateuch is intended. In the eighth chapter, after the account of the taking of Ai, on the confines of Palestine, Joshua is immediately represented as proceeding, with the whole nation of the Israelites, to Mount Ebal in the centre of the enemy's country, (fearless of his foes, and unmolested by them,) and there erecting an altar according to the directions in "the Book of the Law of Moses" (v. 31). The directions referred to are in the twenty-seventh chapter of Deuteronomy; and "the Book of the Law of Moses" must have the same meaning here as the corresponding terms in the passages before quoted. But the narrative immediately goes on to say (vv. 32, 34, 35) that Joshua wrote on the stones of the altar, in the presence of the children of Israel, "a copy of the Law of Moses;" and "afterwards read all the words of the Law, the blessings and cursings, according to all that is written in the Book of the Law. There was not a word of all that Moses commanded, which Joshua read not before all the congregation of Israel." Here, as it is incredible that Joshua should have engraved, or written, the whole Pentateuch on the stones of the altar, it has been imagined by some, that only the book of Deuteronomy was intended; but this is also incredible. Others, therefore, have supposed, that "the Law of Moses" here means only the blessings and cursings recorded in the twenty-seventh and twenty-eight chapters of Deuteronomy. But this is inconsistent with the use of the term, not merely elsewhere, but, as we have seen, in this account itself. These blessings and curses are nowhere else called "the Law of Moses," nor could they be so with propriety. They were the sanctions of the Law, not the Law itself. Beside, it is evident that Joshua read to the people the same which he had written on the altar. Now, according to the directions in Deuteronomy (xxvii. 14), it was not his business, but that of the Levites, to pronounce those blessings and curses. Others, therefore, have thought, that by "the Law of Moses," as here used, the Ten Commandments only are meant. But, beside that this supposition, like that last mentioned, gives a meaning to the term inconsistent with its common use, and especially with its use immediately before, it may be added, that, if the writer had only intended to say, that Joshua read the Ten Commandments, he would hardly have insisted so strongly upon his having read the whole Law, omitting not a word.

The relation, therefore, appears not like the history of a real event, but like the narrative of one who did not well consider what he was writing.

But this account in the Book of Joshua is to be compared with the directions which Moses is represented to have given, in Deuteronomy xxvii. 2-8. On these directions it is founded, and they are liable to similar objections with the account itself. Moses, it is said, ordered, that after the Israelites had passed the Jordan, they should "set up great stones, and plaster them with plaster," "and write upon the stones *all the words of this Law*, very plainly."

"Then, said I, Lo, I come: in the volume of the book* it is written of me."

The meaning of the words is uncertain, and they have been variously rendered and explained. But the passage, however understood, would, at most, prove only, that in the time of David (if he were its writer), that is, according to the common computation, about four centuries after the death of Moses, the Jews possessed some book which they believed to teach what God had prescribed to them. There is no evidence that this book was the Pentateuch. On the contrary, it seems altogether improbable, that it was any book inculcating the ceremonial law of the Jews, as that is laid down in the Pentateuch, considering how the passage is introduced and connected. Such, on the contrary, is the unqualified manner in which it is asserted, that sacrifices were not required by God, that the passage may be considered as affording strong proof, that, at the time when it was written, the Pentateuch did not exist.

" In sacrifice and oblation thou hast no pleasure :
Mine ears thou hast opened : †

By "all the words of this Law," it is clear, from a comparison of many passages in Deuteronomy, in which these or equivalent terms are used, that the author or compiler of that book could have meant *nothing less* than the whole body of laws contained in it. On the supposition, that the book of Deuteronomy originally formed a part of the Pentateuch, and was written by Moses in connection with the other four books, the terms in question must denote the whole Pentateuch. For Moses, it is said (xxxi. 24-26), "made an end of writing *the words of this Law* in a book," and gave it to the Levites to be deposited by the side of the ark of the Covenant, for a witness against the nation. Had he written the whole of the Pentateuch, he would not have separated the book of Deuteronomy from it to be thus preserved alone, as containing the words of the Law. We cannot on that supposition believe that the book, which he gave to the Levites to be thus scrupulously cared for, was not the whole Pentateuch, with the exception, of course, of those portions of it which he could not have written. That it was the whole Pentateuch has generally been admitted, or contended for, by those who have regarded the Pentateuch as the work of Moses.

* The words should be rendered; "in the scroll of the book," meaning simply "the book." The periphrasis (which was perhaps used as a more solemn expression) is founded on the manner in which books were anciently written, in the form of a roll.

† That is, Thou hast made me hear thy voice ; Thou hast enabled me to understand thy will.

Burnt-offering and sin-offering thou dost not desire :
Therefore, I said, Lo, I come:
In the scroll of the book it is written of me:
Oh my God! to do thy will is my delight,
And thy law dwells in my heart." *

*In the scroll of the book it is written of me:* this is a verbal rendering; and in these words it may seem most probable, that the Psalmist did not refer to any book, properly speaking, but to that book, in which, according to an imagination common from his day to our own, God is conceived of as recording both what He sees, and more especially what He wills and purposes,—the book, as it may be called, of the Divine Mind.† He may be understood as saying, Lo! I come, as thou hast written, that is, as thou hast purposed, concerning me.

With the exception of the passages that have been referred to in the Book of Joshua, there is no express mention of a Book of the Law ascribed to Moses in any writing of the Old Testament, which has been supposed to be of an age prior to the Captivity.‡ No such book is mentioned in the Books, or rather Book, of Samuel. By the prophets, the public teachers of religion among the Jews, such a book is nowhere spoken of. No evidence can be drawn from their writings of the existence of the Pentateuch, or of any book ascribed to Moses as its author. The fact is important as

* This version varies a little from that of the Rev. Dr. Noyes ; whose Translations of the Psalms, of Job, and of the Prophets, are, I believe, well entitled to the reputation they enjoy, among those to whom they are known, of being the best in our language.

† See Psalm lvi. 8 ; lxix. 28; lxxxvii. 6 ; cxxxix. 16. Isaiah iv. 3 ; xxxiv. 16 ; lxv. 6. Daniel vii. 10 ; xii. 1. Exod. xxxii. 32, 33. [*See note* A *at the end of the volume.*—ED.]

‡ The Captivity commenced, according to the common computation, in the year 606 before Christ, that is, about eight centuries and a half after the death of Moses.—I except, in the sentence above, the book of Joshua, because that *has been supposed to have been* written before the Captivity, and even by Joshua himself. Nothing can well be more untenable than the latter supposition. The fact, that it was ascribed to him by the same Jewish tradition which has assigned their supposed authors to other parts of the Old Testament, serves to show how little credit that tradition is entitled to. We have no knowledge by whom the book of Joshua was written. Its composition was apparently subsequent to that of Deuteronomy.

regards our present inquiry. It amounts to more than a mere absence of proof, that Moses was the author of the Pentateuch. Considering that the prophets were the public teachers of religion, the fact, that there is no distinct notice in their writings of a book ascribed to the great Lawgiver of the nation, a book which must have been the fundamental document in all that concerned religion, creates a strong suspicion that no such book was in existence, or, as regards the prophets after the Captivity, that no such book had been handed down with the authority of antiquity. What should we think of a series of Christian teachers, from whose works no satisfactory evidence could be deduced of the existence of the New Testament?

We come, then, to the Books of Kings, or rather the Book of Kings, as it should be called, there being no ground for the division either of Samuel, the Kings, or the Chronicles, into two books. Each was reckoned in the Hebrew Canon but as one work. The Book of Kings (to speak of it in the singular number) is brought down to the thirty-seventh year of the Captivity,* about nine centuries, as commonly computed, after the death of Moses. It is unimportant, as it regards our present inquiry, whether it was written, or rather compiled, during the continuance, or after the termination, of the Captivity. Any testimony in this work, did such testimony exist, to the supposed fact, that Moses wrote the Pentateuch nine hundred years before, would be of no weight. But the work contains no testimony to this effect. We find words ascribed to David, as his dying charge to Solomon, in which he exhorts him " to keep all the statutes, commands, decrees, and ordinances of the Lord, as written in the Law of Moses."† The writer speaks in his own person of " what is written in the Law of Moses," quoting a passage to be found only in Deuteronomy.‡ And he gives an account of the discovery in the Temple, by the high-priest Hilkiah, of " the Book of the Law," during

---

\* 2 Kings xxv. 27. † 1 Kings ii. 3.
‡ 2 Kings xiv. 6. Comp. Deut. xxiv. 16.

the reign of Josiah * (B.C. 924, as computed). These and other passages in which "the Law," or "the Law of Moses," is mentioned, prove that before the composition of the Book of the Kings, the Jews possessed a written code of laws, which bore the name of Moses. But, without supposing this code to have been written by Moses, we cannot doubt that, by whomsoever compiled, it included all those precepts and laws which were given, or which the Jews believed to have been given, by him. As many as could by any plausible tradition, or perhaps by any plausible invention, be ascribed to him, would be so ascribed. Additional laws might be represented as mere deductions from those of which he was the real or reputed author. Hence it is easy to understand, why a code of Jewish laws, whenever compiled, should be called the Law of Moses. But the existence of such a code does not prove that the five books of the Pentateuch were written by Moses.

On the contrary, it seems impossible plausibly to reconcile the narrative just referred to, of the discovery in the Temple of a copy of "the Book of the Law," with the supposition, that this book was the Pentateuch, and that the Pentateuch was written by Moses. It is plain that, according to that account, the book was before unknown to Josiah, a religious prince, to his secretary Shaphan, and to the high-priest Hilkiah. It cannot, therefore, be supposed, that the existence of such a book was known to any of the higher officers of the State, or to any of the principal priests; and if, during a religious reign, which had continued for eighteen years, it was unknown to them, we cannot reasonably suppose that it was known to any one, or, to say the least, that it was generally known. But the Pentateuch, if written by Moses, was the most venerable and valuable possession of the nation, and an object of the highest interest, not only to every religious man, but to every Jew not destitute of the love of his country, or a sense of the true honour of his people. It was the work in which the Law-giver of the

* 2 Kings xxii. 8, seqq.

nation, the messenger of God, had related the wonderful events of his own ministry, and announced those ordinances which God had appointed through him. It was not merely the proper foundation of the religion and polity of the State; it was in itself the national code of laws, civil and ceremonial. It is difficult to believe that such a book should have been so forgotten. It had survived the long period (about three centuries, as commonly supposed), of anarchy, barbarism, and subjugation, following the death of Joshua. If it had ever been recognized and honoured as the work of Moses, it must have been so in the age of Solomon. From his reign to that of Josiah was a period of somewhere about three centuries and a half. According to the history, the kings of Judah, during the larger part of this time, maintained the national religion. If these kings knew and regarded an express ordinance contained in the Pentateuch,* they had each made a copy of it. If they knew and obeyed another requisition, they had caused it to be read to the assembled people every Sabbatical year.† We have, indeed, good reason to believe that this had not been done; for, as we shall hereafter have occasion to remark, the Sabbatical years had not been observed. But, had the Pentateuch been in existence and regarded as the work of Moses, it cannot be supposed, that, during the long periods when the kings of Judah "did right in the sight of the Lord," they took no effectual means of making known to the people the fundamental book of their religion, and the code of laws which they were bound to obey, or that there were not many among the priests, the prophets, and the better sort of the nation, who were always interested in its study and preservation. We may compare the period of less than four centuries between the reigns of Solomon and Josiah, with the period of fourteen centuries, which intervened between the destruction of Jerusalem and the first printing of the Pentateuch. During this time, the Jews, though scattered among their enemies, and everywhere trampled down by hatred and cruelty, pre-

---

\* Deuteronomy xvii. 18. † Ibid. xxxi. 10, 11.

served, even amid the barbarism of the dark ages, copies of what they then considered as the work of Moses, though few only of their number were able to read it. But, according to the narrative in the Book of Kings, if we suppose it to relate to the Pentateuch, and suppose the Pentateuch to be the work of Moses, it would appear that this work, carrying with it the authority of God, and of the highest interest to the nation, had been so little valued, and had fallen into such oblivion, that, but for an accident, or an interposition of Providence, it might have perished from men's knowledge; and this, though other works written before the Captivity were preserved, and though there had been for two centuries a succession of prophets in Judah and Israel, whose works escaped such neglect.

It follows, therefore, as I conceive, that, whatever were the book produced in the reign of Josiah, it could not have been the Pentateuch, if the Pentateuch were the work of Moses. But, if it were any other book, the Pentateuch was not then in existence, or not considered as the work of Moses; for, had it been in existence and so considered, no other book would have been entitled "the Book of the Law," and produced for the regulation of the national religion.

The book actually produced was, according to the narrative concerning it, a body of laws, professedly resting on divine authority. It may have been one of the documents afterwards made use of in the formation of the Pentateuch. Perhaps it was, as some have conjectured, the book of Deuteronomy, or perhaps it was a book which afterwards served for the basis of that work. It was brought forward to aid the reformation from idolatry under Josiah; and the story of its being accidentally found in the Temple may be thought to have been what was considered a justifiable artifice, to account for the appearance of a book hitherto unknown.

In tracing our course downward from Moses we have now arrived at the period of the re-establishment of the

D

Jews in Palestine, after the Captivity, the period to which we have before ascended. It is unnecessary to examine critically any supposed notices of the Pentateuch in the books of the Old Testament written after that event. · We have seen, that, when the Book of Kings was written, a code of national laws was extant, ascribed to Moses; and those supposed notices prove nothing more.

On reviewing the ground we have gone over, it may appear that no direct historical evidence exists, that the Pentateuch was the work of Moses. But it may be said, that there is strong indirect evidence for this supposition, in the fact, that from the time of Moses the Levitical Law was regarded by the Jews as their national law; that its religious rites were observed by them, its festivals celebrated, and all its statutes, civil and criminal, considered as binding, except when the nation fell into sin and idolatry.

In such statements much is assumed which cannot be proved. It appears, that before the Captivity there was a temple at Jerusalem, and priests and Levites, and sacrifices, and other religious rites; but it does not appear, that the Levitical Law had been, from the time of Moses, the national law of the Jews. On the contrary, there is much that is inconsistent with this supposition.

In proof of it we must not argue from books written after the return of the Jews to Palestine, when we may suppose the Pentateuch to have been in existence, and the Levitical Law to have been established. From the circumstances of the case, the evidence, direct or indirect, which they may seem to afford, is altogether questionable. I refer particularly to the Books of Ezra, Nehemiah, Malachi, and the Chronicles. The compiler of the Chronicles, especially, seems to have given a strong colouring to the ancient history of his nation, derived from the feelings, customs, and institutions of his own age, for the purpose of recommending the Levitical Law to his countrymen by the supposed example and authority of their ancestors. His work appears to have been founded principally on the Books of

Samuel and the Kings; or, to say the least, there is no probability, that, in the portion of his history coincident with what is contained in those books, he had any other authentic documents than what their authors possessed. But in comparing the accounts in those books with the accounts in the Chronicles, we see at once how much the author of this later work has added concerning priests and Levites, and religious ceremonies. As a single illustration of the general character of his work we may take the narrative of the removal of the ark by David to Jerusalem, in the thirteenth, fifteenth, and sixteenth chapters of the first Book of Chronicles, as compared with the account in the sixth chapter of the second Book of Samuel. In the Chronicles the priests and Levites play a principal part. In the Book of Samuel they do not appear at all. The ark is not borne by Levites, as it should have been, according to the Levitical Law, and, contrary to that Law, the sacrifices are offered not by priests but by David.*

Without entering into any critical inquiry, but receiving the accounts of the earlier Jewish historians, as they lie before us, it is evident, that, from the death of Joshua to the time when David proposed to erect a national temple, (a period, as computed, of about four centuries,) there could have been, consistently with the accounts in the Books of Judges and of Samuel, no regular observance of the Levitical Law by the Jewish nation. Nor in the interval between

---

\* The character of the Book of Chronicles, as stated above, was first, I believe, distinctly pointed out and illustrated by De Wette, in his "Critical Essay on the Credibility of the Books of the Chronicles" (in German). Though one may be far from assenting to all that is said by De Wette, yet what is essential in his positions respecting the Chronicles seems to be satisfactorily established; and if so, this work cannot be considered as trustworthy, where it varies from the earlier historians, or adds to their accounts.

In the first part of his Antiquities of the Jews, Josephus could have had no other good authority, than the books of the Old Testament. His work, therefore, affords an example of the licence with which a Jewish historian might remodel and add to the history of his countrymen; and we have no reason to be surprised, if we find a similar character in the earlier author of the Chronicles. [*See note* B *at the end of the volume.*—ED.]

the time when Solomon fell into idolatry\* and the time of the Captivity could this law have been uniformly respected by the Jews as their national law; considering the separation of the people into two kingdoms, which was contrary to it, and the frequent occurrence of idolatrous kings, during whose reigns it must, if it existed, have been in abeyance. In the time of Josiah, as we have seen, "the Book of the Law" was generally unknown; and the apparently accidental discovery of such a book (less than twenty years, as computed, before the commencement of the Captivity) is represented as a momentous event leading to the re-establishment of the national religion.

It is to be observed, that these obvious facts are not adduced to disprove the antiquity of the Levitical Law; they are only brought forward to show, that no proof of its being derived from Moses can be founded on the supposition, that it was the national law of the Jews from the time of Moses. Of this supposition no satisfactory evidence exists; for, as has been remarked, we cannot rely on the historical books written after the Captivity, when the Levitical Law was in operation; for these books were, to all appearance, conformed to the opinions and feelings of this later time. But there is not only a want of satisfactory evidence in proof of the supposition; there is, beside the leading facts that have been mentioned, other direct evidence to the contrary, to which we will now advert.

The author of the Book of Kings relates, that after the discovery of the Book of the Law, in the reign of Josiah, a passover was celebrated in Jerusalem, and adds: "Such a passover had not been kept from the days of the Judges, who judged Israel, nor in all the days of the kings of Israel, nor of the kings of Judah."† With the exception of what is

---

\* Among the many similar facts, which characterize the Book of Chronicles as a work adapted to the opinions and feelings of the Jews after the Captivity, when the Levitical Law was established, it may be observed that it omits all mention of the idolatry of Solomon.

† 2 Kings xxiii. 22.

found in the Pentateuch itself, this is the only mention of the keeping of a passover in any historical book of earlier date than the Chronicles; nor is there in the Prophets who wrote before the Captivity, any distinct allusion to what afterwards became the great national festival. If the writer of the Book of Kings meant to say, that so splendid a passover had not been celebrated before, not even in the days of Solomon, this would be almost equivalent to saying, that no passover had been celebrated at all. If his meaning were, that the rites of the ceremonial Law were more strictly observed than they had been before, the remark must imply, that they were then for the first time fully observed since the days of the Judges.

In the Book of Nehemiah, written more than a thousand years after the death of Moses, there is a mention of the celebration of the Feast of Tabernacles;* and, in speaking of it, the writer says, " Since the days of Joshua the son of Nun to that day had not the children of Israel done so." " We see," says the learned Joseph Mede,† " how expressly this Feast of Tabernacles was commanded yearly to be observed. Nevertheless, which is past all belief, it was never kept, at least in this main circumstance of *dwelling in booths* from the time of Joshua till after their return from Captivity." Le Clerc‡ remarks, that "this law [the law respecting the Feast of Tabernacles] was neither obscure nor hard to be observed. But, as I have often said, the laws of Moses were never accurately observed." The national festivals, appointed by a ceremonial law, are of all its ordinances the least likely to be neglected.

The writer of the Book of Chronicles himself gives us to understand,§ that the seventy years of the Captivity answered to seventy Sabbatical years which had not been kept. If, as is implied in what is said, the Sabbatical year had not been

---

\* Nehemiah, ch. viii. Comp. Ezra iii. 4-6, which I suppose to relate to the same celebration.
† Discourse xlviii. Works, p. 268. Ed. 1679.
‡ Comment. in loc. § 2 Chron. xxxvi. 21.

observed for between four and five centuries preceding the Captivity, that is, for more than five centuries before the time of the writer, there is little reason to believe that any evidence then existed of its ever having been observed. With the Sabbatical years, the years of Jubilee were intimately connected, and if there were no Sabbatical years, we cannot reasonably suppose that there were any years of Jubilee. Yet the laws regarding the Sabbatical year and the Jubilee are among the most important of those concerning the rights of property, and, at the same time, are represented to have been intimately interwoven with the theocratical government of the Jews, as implying a periodical miracle.

According to a law in Leviticus,\* it was enjoined under a severe penalty, that sacrifices should be offered only where the Tabernacle was placed. According to another law in Deuteronomy,† after the Jews were established in Palestine, one place of national worship was to be designated, where alone sacrifices were to be offered. This one place was to be considered as the habitation of Jehovah, where alone the people were to seek Him and come before Him. These laws are apparently fundamental among those relating to the public worship. There is a narrative in the Book of Joshua,‡ according to which their obligation was recognized. But it does not appear elsewhere from the early Jewish history, extending down to the building of Solomon's temple, that such laws existed. On the contrary, altars were raised and sacrifices offered by holy men in various places, and in places where the Tabernacle was not; and such facts are related without censure by the historian.

Thus, for example.—In the first chapter of the first Book of Samuel, we find the Tabernacle and the Ark, with Eli and his sons, at Shiloh. Here was the house of Jehovah. The Ark being taken, and afterwards restored, by the Philistines, it was left at Kirjath-jearim, where Eleazar, the son of Abinadab, was consecrated to keep it. Here it appears to have been suffered to remain, separated from the Tabernacle,

---

\* Ch. xvii. 3-9. † Ch. xii. 2-14. ‡ Ch. xxii. 10-31.

for the greater part of the time, during nearly half a century, till David removed it to Jerusalem. At one period, during this interval, it appears,\* that the Tabernacle, with priests, was at Nob, where undoubtedly sacrifices were offered. Meanwhile, Samuel, the prophet of Jehovah, called the people together before the Lord at Mizpeh, and, though not a priest, offered a burnt-offering.† He built an altar to Jehovah at Ramah, the place of his residence.‡ He assisted at a sacrifice on a high place, somewhere in the land of Zuph.§ He proposed to offer sacrifices at Gilgal.|| He again called the people before Jehovah at Mizpeh.¶ The people, under his direction, re-acknowledged Saul as king before Jehovah at Gilgal, where they offered peace-offerings.\*\* Bethel was another place where Jehovah was sought.†† And, not to multiply instances unnecessarily, we afterwards find mention of a grandson of Eli, " the Lord's priest in Shiloh, wearing an ephod."‡‡

The author of the Book of Kings, speaking of the state of things at the commencement of Solomon's reign, says,§§ " The people sacrificed on high places; because there was no house built to the Lord until these days." " Although, says Le Clerc,|||| " according to the law in Leviticus, sacrifices ought to have been offered only where the Tabernacle was placed, yet that law had not hitherto been observed, nor was this imputed to the people as an offence." Solomon himself, it is related, " went to sacrifice at Gibeon; for that was the great high place;" and so far, according to the narrative, was his conduct from being blameable, that the Lord there gave him the choice of whatever blessings he might desire.

It is true, that in relation to these facts, and others of the same kind, it may be said, that we cannot infer that a

---

\* 1 Samuel, ch. xxi. xxii.
† Ibid. vii. 5. 9.
‡ Ibid. vii. 17.
§ Ibid. ix. 5, 12, 13.
|| Ibid. x. 8.
¶ 1 Sam. x. 17.
\*\* Ibid. xi. 15.
†† Ibid. x. 3.
‡‡ Ibid. xiv. 3.
§§ 1 Kings iii. 2.
|||| Comment. in loc.

law is not extant from the circumstance of its not being obeyed; that all laws are, more or less, disregarded and transgressed; that Moses was often disobeyed in his lifetime, and that, therefore, the Levitical Law may have existed and may have proceeded from Moses, though it was disobeyed in all the instances that have been mentioned. The force of these general remarks is, however, invalidated, when we consider that the instances of supposed disobedience relate to ordinances most likely to be observed, as those concerning the celebration of festivals; to statutes essentially affecting the rights of property, and sanctioned by the promise of a regular interposition of God,* as those concerning the Sabbatical year and the Jubilee; and to laws apparently fundamental in the national worship, as those directing a single place to be fixed upon for the celebration of its rites; and, we may add, though the fact has not been dwelt upon before, those appointing the priests to be the sole ministers in offering sacrifices. The case becomes more striking when we find that these laws, supposing them in being, were not only disregarded, but disregarded without censure, by men who are represented as having been highly favoured by the Lord.

But it is to be kept in mind, that it is not the proper purpose of these remarks directly to prove that the Levitical Law was not given by Moses. Perhaps the supposition, that it was given by Moses, may be reconcilable with all the facts that have been stated. The purpose of the preceding remarks has merely been to show, that the supposed fact, that the Levitical Law in its present state was from the time of Moses the national Law of the Jews, cannot be rendered probable; and, therefore, that this supposed fact can afford no proof towards establishing the proposition, that Moses was the author of the Pentateuch.

* "And if ye ask, What shall we eat during the seventh year, seeing we must not sow nor gather in our increase? I answer, I will command my blessing upon you in the sixth year, and it shall bring forth produce for three years."—Leviticus xxv. 20, 21.

From the examination we have gone through of the books of the Old Testament, it may appear that the existence of the Pentateuch, as we now possess it, cannot be traced, by any historical evidence, beyond the return of the Jews from their Captivity. According to a Jewish tradition before quoted,* they possessed on their return no copy of the Pentateuch. This tradition flattered none of their prejudices concerning it, and no national feeling; and this circumstance affords some presumption, that it was founded on truth. It is such a tradition as might naturally arise, if the compilation and fashioning of the Pentateuch were subsequent to the Captivity; and one of which no account can be given, if this were not the fact.

If, indeed, the Pentateuch were not written by Moses, perhaps we cannot with probability assign to it, in its present form, an earlier date than some time after the return of the Jews from their Captivity. When restored to Palestine, their national polity was to be re-established; they were again to be formed into a State. To effect this end, it was requisite that a written code of laws should be provided. In forming such a code their ancient laws would naturally be revived. Some, perhaps, were inserted, of which only a traditional story existed, and which, it is not probable, ever had been, or ever were subsequently, observed; such, for example, as the law respecting the Sabbatical year.† New

---

* See pp. 22, 23.

† I, of course, attach no credit to the story of Josephus (Antiq. Jud. Lib. xi. cap. 8, § 5) respecting the remission of the tribute of every seventh year, obtained by the Jews from Alexander, which he apparently means to imply was on account of their observance of the Sabbatical years. His whole narrative concerning Alexander's interview with the Jewish high-priest, and of his favour to the Jewish nation, is unquestionably fabulous. It shows this character on its very face; and it has been made evident by Moyle, and others, that it will bear no critical examination. See Moyle's Correspondence with Prideaux, in the second volume of his Works, p. 26, seqq. Mitford's History of Greece, ch. xlviii. § 4, note 16.—Mitford, through some mistake, says that the story is told also "in the book of Maccabees."

Josephus is not a writer to be trusted in any questionable case. It may be worth while to produce a single other illustration of his character, in a matter of some curiosity, which has not, so far as I know, been before brought to

laws, we may suppose, were added to the old; and ceremonies, there is little doubt, were multiplied. At the same time, a strong national feeling must have revived among the Jews, together with a sense of their peculiar relation to God. The history of that dispensation which allied them to God would thus become an object of great interest. All traditions concerning it, written and oral, would be sought out and preserved. The laws of the nation would be ascribed, as far as possible, to their divinely-commissioned Lawgiver; and for this it is not unlikely that some remaining book or books of their ancient laws, as well as the current of tradition, afforded abundant pretence. Thus, from written documents, and oral traditions, we may suppose the Pentateuch to have been compiled by some of those who held the highest authority in the new State. Such a book, or rather, such a collection of books, under the circumstances of the time, and with the excited feelings of the people, would be readily received. If some fabrications proceeded from the compilers, we should be slow, considering the state of ancient morality, and the loose notions of truth then prevailing, to bring this as a very grave charge against them. That the books were originally ascribed to Moses as their author is highly improbable; for, if their compilers had had any intention of representing him as their author, they would naturally have made him speak in the first person, and they would not have introduced the various passages which, it is obvious, at the first glance, that he could not have written, as, for example, the account of his own death. But the

notice. Making a computation from the number of lambs sacrificed at the passover, he seems to imply, that the number of Jews who had assembled at Jerusalem to celebrate the passover, and who were shut up in the city when besieged by Titus, was more than two millions and a half. But, putting aside this larger number, he expressly asserts, that those who *perished* in the siege were eleven hundred thousand. (De Bello Jud. Lib. vi. c. 9.) The walls of the city, he elsewhere says (Ibid. Lib. v. c. 4, § 3), were thirty-three stadia in circumference. They, therefore, included less than one square mile. But a square mile, if levelled, and free from buildings and thoroughfares, would have afforded for each of the eleven hundred thousand persons, for himself, his furniture, utensils, provisions, and arms, a place of but a little more than five feet square.

Pentateuch was called "the Book of Moses;" and in this, as in numberless other cases, the ambiguity of language may have led into error. This title, meaning a book contaiug the history and laws of Moses, might easily, in process of time, in an uncritical age and ·nation, come to be interpreted as signifying a book written by Moses. The belief that he was the author of the whole of the Pentateuch was undoubtedly greatly facilitated by the fact, that he is represented in it as having committed much or the whole of the Levitical Law to writing, and by the readiness with which a supposition would be admitted, which ascribed a book of such a character to the inspired Lawgiver of the nation.

Such may have been the origin of the Pentateuch, supposing it not to be the work of Moses. But it is to be recollected, that the main question before us is not, whether this particular hypothesis concerning its formation be probable, but whether it was written by Moses. In support of the proposition, that he was its author, there is, as we have seen, properly speaking, no historical evidence. In all common cases this fact would be decisive of the question; since it would be wholly unreasonable to ascribe a work to a particular author, when we have no evidence that it was ascribed to him before a thousand years after his death. Whether this case be an extraordinary one, to which peculiar proof is applicable, is a question to which we shall hereafter attend, so far as is necessary. But it may here be recollected, that in our search for historical evidence, we have not only seen that such evidence is wanting, but have found reasons for believing that the books in question were not written by Moses. For it is not credible that these books, if written by Moses, and carrying with them the authority of God, should not have been appealed to by the prophets, the public teachers of the religion of God, who ought to have made them the basis of their instructions. Nor is it credible, that they should have come so near perishing, as to be saved only by a providential discovery, just before the nation fell into ruin and captivity. The tradition of the Jews, that no copy of them was extant on the return of the nation from their Captivity, favours much more the supposition, that they had their origin after that event, than the supposition which ascribes them to Moses. And if it appear that, before that event fundamental ordinances of the Levitical Law were not observed, and even that individuals specially favoured by Heaven acted contrary to them without censure from God or man, it affords a presumption, more or less strong, that the Levitical Law had not God for its author, nor Moses for the organ of its communication.

## SECTION IV.

#### SOME GENERAL CONSIDERATIONS RESPECTING THE AUTHORSHIP OF THE PENTATEUCH.

It may appear, then, from what has been said, that there is no historical evidence, that the Pentateuch was written by Moses; but, on the contrary, that the Jewish history affords proof that he was not its author. We will now pass to some general considerations by which the same conclusion seems to be established.

I. According to the common computation Moses lived in the fifteenth century before Christ. Such, however, I conceive to be the uncertainty of the early Jewish history and chronology, that no approach to accuracy can be made in fixing the time when he lived. But, though it may have been earlier, it, probably, was not much later than the period just mentioned; and in assuming this as correct we shall commit no error which will affect our reasoning.

There is, then, no satisfactory evidence that alphabetical writing was known at this period. If known to others, it is improbable that it was known to the Hebrews. And, in any case, there is no reason to suppose, that they were so familiar with its use, that a book, and especially that five such books as compose the Pentateuch, might have been written for their instruction. Such books are not written except for a people among whom there are many readers. The injunctions, likewise, respecting the use of writing in the Pentateuch,* imply that the Jews, at the time when they were given, were familiarly acquainted with it; and so also does the reference, which it contains, to another book, "The Book of the Wars of the Lord,"† as already in existence.

But it must have been long after the first rudiments of alphabetical writing had been attained, before the invention was brought to a state so nearly complete, as that in which it appears in the Hebrew alphabet. It must have been a still longer time, before an acquaintance with it had become so common, as to lead to its use for the purpose of communicating instruction by books. Probably it was first used in inscriptions, and in committing to writing compositions principally metrical, which had already become familiar by oral tradition. In the latter case, the intended significance of the newly-discovered signs being already known, they would be easily deciphered, and the art of reading would thus be gradually spread. Books, like those which form the Pentateuch, in prose, and in a style so well constructed, must have been comparatively a very late result of the invention. But, if we suppose Moses to have been the author of the Pentateuch, we must suppose, that before his time the art of writing was in common use, and the consequent demand for the materials employed in it so great, as to render them of very easy acquisition; for Moses must either have provided himself prospectively with a large store of them in the haste of his departure from Egypt, or have afterwards obtained them in the deserts of Arabia. But for a long time after the supposed date of the Pentateuch we find no proof of the existence of a book, or even of an inscription, in proper alphabetical characters among the nations by whom the Hebrews were surrounded.‡

The descendants of Jacob, according to their history, resided not less than two hundred and fifteen years in Egypt.

* Deut. vi. 9; xi. 20; xxiv. 1. † Numbers xxi. 14.
‡ [See note c at the end of the volume.—ED.]

During this time they could not have learned alphabetical writing from the Egyptians; for the mode of representing ideas to the eye, which the Egyptians employed till a period long subsequent, was widely different from the alphabetical writing of the Hebrews. Nor is it probable, that the descendants of Jacob, who were first shepherds and then slaves in Egypt, were the inventors of the art. If they were acquainted with it, they must, it would seem, have brought it with them into the country. But we can hardly suppose, that it was invented, or acquired except by tradition, in the family of Isaac, or in that of Jacob before his residence in Egypt, engaged as they both were in agriculture and the care of cattle. We must then go back to Abraham at least for what traditionary knowledge of it his descendants in Egypt may be supposed to have possessed. But it would be idle to argue against the supposition, that alphabetical writing was known in the time of Abraham.

II. We proceed to another consideration. The vocabulary and style of the Pentateuch cannot have been the vocabulary and style of Moses. There is no important difference between the Hebrew of the Pentateuch and that of the other books of the Old Testament, written before the re-establishment of the Jews in Palestine after their Captivity. But from the time of Moses to this event was an interval of about nine hundred or a thousand years. Every other language, the history of which we can trace, if it have continued a living language, has undergone great changes during the same or a shorter period; as, for instance, the English, during the four centuries and a half since the days of Wicliff and Chaucer, and the Latin, in a still shorter interval between the laws of the Twelve Tables and the time of Cicero. But the language of the Israelites was peculiarly exposed to change during the long period of its existence as a spoken tongue after the time of Moses. Its vocabulary, never copious, must have been originally barren; accommodated to the wants of a people having but a narrow sphere of thought. It must not only have enlarged itself to receive

the new accession of religious conceptions communicated by
Moses ; but must have been afterward in a state of continual growth, to adapt itself to the subsequent intellectual
development of the Hebrews, and to the most extraordinary
circumstances in which they were placed by the new dispensation. After the death of Moses, they established
themselves in a new country, widely different in its natural
aspect from Egypt ;—from being slaves employed in making
bricks, they became accustomed to the use of arms ;—they
were placed in new relations, and became familiar with new
objects and new customs. They were pressed upon by other
nations, speaking, as we have reason to believe, languages
or dialects different from their own, with whom they intermingled, whose idolatrous rites, and other customs,' they
sometimes adopted, and to whom, in the earlier part of their
history, they were sometimes in servitude. Their engaging
in commerce in the time of Solomon must have had its
customary effect to give a new colouring to their speech.
Before the time of Samuel, they were wholly without that
attention to literature, and that intellectual cultivation, which
might have served to fix their language, and certainly had
no literary watchfulness to guard against its corruption ; nor
can we suppose that those habits of mind existed in a high
degree during any stage of their history. Under such circumstances a language cannot remain the same for nine or
ten centuries. The supposition, that the Pentateuch in its
present form was written by Moses, is as untenable as would
be the supposition, that some book written in modern English
was a composition of the age of Chaucer. The attempts
which have been made to point out certain archaisms of style
in the Pentateuch, only show that no evidence can be produced of such peculiarity of language as the case requires.*

* In treating of the perfection of the Hebrew language, Leusden, one of
the most learned Hebrew scholars of his time, thus writes :—" The uniformity
of the Hebrew language in all the books of the Old Testament contributes
much to its perfection. I have often wondered that there should be so great
a correspondence between the Hebrew of all the books of the Old Testament,
when we know that they were composed by different men (whose respective
styles of writing are often distinguishable), at diverse times, and in diverse
places. Should a book be written by different men of the same city, we should

Nor is the existence of those supposed archaisms difficult to be accounted for. The Pentateuch, if not the work of Moses, was undoubtedly, in great part, a compilation; and from the pre-existing documents or traditions which formed its basis those few antiquated or peculiar forms of speech might be copied or imitated.

III. In the next place, it may be observed, that the Pentateuch contains passages, which, it is agreed, could not have been written by Moses. Some of them are obvious to every reader; as, for instance, the account of his own death, and the passage in Genesis,* in which it is said, "These are the kings who reigned in the land of Edom, before there

perceive for the most part greater differences in it, as respects style or orthography, or some other circumstances, than appear in the whole Old Testament. But let a book be written by a German and by a Frieslander, or let there be an interval of a thousand years between the writers, as there was between many of those of the Old Testament, what a difference of language would appear! He who understood the writing of one might scarcely understand that of the other. Nay, the difference of time and place would render their modes of speech so unlike, that it would be very difficult to apply to them the same rules of grammar and syntax. But in the Old Testament there is so great a uniformity, such a correspondence in orthography and construction, that one might almost think that all the books were written at the same time and in the same place, though by different authors."—Philologus Hebræus, Diss. xvii. pp. 166, 167.

It is the opinion of Gesenius, the most distinguished Hebrew scholar of our day, that the antiquity of the Hebrew language, *in its present form*, hardly reaches higher than the age of David or Solomon. "Upon the supposition," he says, "that the Pentateuch was a production of the age of Moses, we must indeed carry its existence back to a period considerably more remote. But notwithstanding the learned defenders which that supposition has found in our own age, it can scarcely approve itself to the judgment of an unprejudiced critic. . . . . It is a fact, that the language of the Pentateuch fully corresponds with that of the other ancient historical books, and, in the poetical portions, with that of the other poetry of the first age." [Gesenius considers the first age of the Hebrew language as extending to the time when it was corrupted by the influence of the Chaldee in consequence of the Captivity.] "If there was an interval of nearly a thousand years between these writings, as there must have been on the supposition that Moses was the author of the Pentateuch, a phenomenon would be presented to which there is nothing parallel in the whole history of language, namely, that the living language of a people, and the circle of their ideas, should remain so unaltered for such a length of time."—Geschichte der Hebräischen Sprache und Schrift: *i. e.* History of the Hebrew Language and Modes of Writing, § 8.

* Ch. xxxvi. 31.

reigned any king over the children of Israel." But such passages, it is said, do not prove that the Pentateuch was not his work; they are to be regarded only as additions made to it by some later hand. To this, it may be answered, that there is a presumption, that a work is not to be ascribed to a particular individual, when it contains a considerable number of passages which he obviously could not have written, though this presumption, undoubtedly, may be overborne by opposite evidence. It may be remarked, likewise, that upon the supposition that Moses was the writer of the Pentateuch, there would have been a natural reluctance among the Hebrews to making or permitting such useless interpolations; to thus tampering with a work so venerable, the composition of their inspired lawgiver, recording the very words of God himself; their infallible directory in religion and morals, and the unalterable code of their civil law. A book thus unique might be expected to escape corruption. During the period concerning which we have satisfactory evidence that the Pentateuch has been so regarded by the Jews, we know that such interpolations have not been made in it. But it is unnecessary to insist on these considerations; there is another to be attended to. At the time when those supposed interpolations were made, no importance could have been attached to the belief, that the Pentateuch was written by Moses. The necessary effect of such interpolations was to incorporate into the book itself evidence,—false evidence, it may be said, but still evidence, and such as appears at first view decisive,—that the book was not written by him. Those, therefore, by whom the interpolations were introduced could not have attached any importance to a belief, which they took such means to destroy. But to say that no importance was attached to the belief that the Pentateuch was written by Moses, is but saying in other words, that it did not exist; for it is impossible, if the belief existed, that it should not have been considered as essentially affecting the character and authority of the Pentateuch.

IV. There is another consideration. The books of the

Pentateuch do not claim to be the work of Moses. They profess to contain his history, but they are not professedly written by him.

The fact has been regarded as of little weight; because in other historical works, as in those of Cæsar and Clarendon, the author has spoken of himself in the third person. But this is a deviation from common usage and the natural mode of expression, occasioned by some particular motive. It may be adopted by a writer in order to avoid an air of arrogance or vanity; or to give the appearance of impartiality to his history; as if it were unaffected by his personal feelings; or to place himself under the same point of view with other individuals whom he introduces into his narrative. It is a mode of writing which belongs not to a rude, but to a refined age; and no probable reason can be assigned why it should have been adopted by Moses. Such a semblance of modesty would have been wholly unsuitable to his office. As the minister of God to his countrymen, it was his business to speak with authority, to assert his claims to deference, and to place himself without reserve before them, as one whom they were bound to listen to and obey.

But the fact is of much importance under another aspect. Did the Pentateuch assume to be the work of Moses, then, in denying it to be his work, we should be driven to the supposition of intentional fraud. But this would be the supposition not merely of a very gross imposture, but of an imposture which, as regards such books, ascribed to such an author, was very unlikely to be attempted, and very unlikely to be successful. On the other hand, there is no difficulty in supposing that a series of books might at any time be readily received by the Jews, which, without claiming to be the work of Moses, embodied the traditions respecting their ancient history, and those that had long been gathering round his name, and which referred to him as their author those laws, that had been gradually built up on the basis of his institutions.

## SECTION V.

ON THE INTERNAL CHARACTER OF THE PENTATEUCH.

THE arguments hitherto adduced do not involve the credibility of the narratives contained in the Pentateuch, or any moral or religious considerations. It is different with those about to be stated.

In judging whether the Pentateuch be the work of Moses, that is, of a writer deserving the highest credit, we must consider whether the narratives it contains are in themselves credible. These narratives may be divided into two classes, those which relate to natural and those which relate to supernatural events. As regards either class, it may be sufficient to direct attention to the subject, and then leave it to every one's private investigation and thought. Of many examples a few may be adduced, which seem to show that the history cannot be regarded as authentic, nor as the work of a contemporary of the supposed events which it narrates. We will first attend to those narratives which concern events not miraculous.

I. The number of fighting men among the Israelites ("every male from twenty years old and upward"), immediately after their leaving Egypt, is said to have been more than six hundred thousand; the numbers of each tribe being particularly given.* This statement of the whole sum of the fighting men is repeatedly made.† It included none from the tribe of Levi, who did not go forth to war. The whole number of the Israelites, therefore, at the time of their leaving Egypt, cannot be estimated at less than two millions and a half. More than eighty years before the time of their departure, a king of Egypt is represented as saying, " Lo ! the people of the children of Israel are more numerous and

* Numbers i. 19-46.
† Numbers ii. 32 ; xi. 21 ; xxvi. 51. Exod. xii. 37 ; xxxviii. 26.

stronger than we." The land of Egypt is said to have been filled with them.* Let us consider this account of their numbers.

The Israelites who established themselves in Egypt, that is, Jacob and his descendants, are stated, in the Books of Genesis and Exodus, to have been seventy in number.† To these, in reckoning the progenitors of the nation, must be added the wives of his sons and grandsons. Their number is uncertain, but, as only two of his grandsons are mentioned as having children at this time, if we assume that the progenitors of the Israelites amounted to two hundred, the whole error in our estimate must be through excess. No one who receives the accounts in Genesis and Exodus as authentic, can suppose that the number was greater.

How long, then, did the Israelites remain in Egypt? There are two different opinions on the subject; according to one of which, the period of their residence was two hundred and fifteen years, and according to the other, four hundred and thirty. Passing over some critical considerations, which bear upon the question, there are others that may enable us to form a judgment respecting it. It cannot be believed, that the Israelites would have remained a distinct people among the Egyptians for four hundred and thirty years. Four hundred and thirty years are a sixth part of that period, beyond which darkness and uncertainty settle upon the whole history of mankind. When we look back to the changes that have taken place since the commencement of the fifteenth century of our era, we may have some notion of what is likely to occur during such a length of time. After the Jews had been separated by God from the rest of the men through the ministry of Moses, their religion might prevent them from mixing with other nations. But while they were in Egypt there was no permanent ob-

* Exod. i. 7, 9.
† Genesis xlvi. 5-27. Exodus i. 5. Stephen, in his speech (Acts vii. 14), says "seventy-five," following the Septuagint. It has been supposed, that to make this number the five grandsons of Joseph, who were born after the establishment of Jacob's family in Egypt, are added.

stacle to their becoming incorporated with the Egyptians as one people; and in the nature of things such an incorporation would have taken place in the course of four centuries.

Upon their leaving Egypt, we find that all the descendants of each of the twelve sons of Jacob could severally be referred to their respective progenitors. The nation could readily be divided into twelve tribes. But we can hardly suppose this to have been possible after an interval of four centuries. When established in Canaan, there may have been particular reasons for their preserving their family genealogies, but there was none before. They were in the same circumstances in this respect as the generality of men in other nations; and in what other nation have the individuals who compose it been able to trace back their genealogy for four hundred years, each to a particular son of a common ancestor?

But the genealogy of Moses may alone seem decisive of the question. Moses, on his mother's side, is stated to have been the grandson of Levi. "The name of Amram's wife was Jochebed, a daughter of Levi, whom her mother bare to Levi in Egypt: and she bare unto Amram, Aaron, and Moses, and Miriam, their sister."\* It has been suggested, that by "a daughter of Levi" may be meant nothing more than "a woman of the tribe of Levi." But the probability of this interpretation may be tested by substituting the latter words for the former, in the passage before us: "The name of Amram's wife was Jochebed, a woman of the tribe of Levi, whom her mother bore to Levi in Egypt." According to the explanation proposed, the last clause is worse than a mere useless repetition. It perplexes the sense. The assertion, that "the mother of Jochebed bore her to Levi" can mean only what the writer is supposed to have just said, that Jochebed *was of the tribe of Levi;* and the addition, that she bore her "in Egypt," becomes altogether idle. But if there were any doubt about the meaning of this passage, it would be settled by another in Exodus,† where it is said,

\* Numbers xxvi. 59.      † Ch. vi. 16, 20.

that Kohath was the son of Levi, and that Amram was the son of Kohath, and thus the grandson of Levi; and that "Amram took him to wife Jochebed, his father's sister," who was consequently Levi's daughter, "and she bare him Aaron and Moses." The statement of the same fact, that Jochebed, the mother of Moses, was the daughter of Levi, in these two different forms, can leave no question as to the meaning of the writer. Yet about eighty years before the Israelites left Egypt, Jochebed was capable of bearing children; for Moses is said to have been eighty years old when he spoke to Pharaoh.* As Moses was on his mother's side the grandson of Levi, so he was on his father's side the grandson of Kohath, who was born before the Israelites entered Egypt.† Upon the supposition that the Pentateuch was written by him, it is to be recollected that this is his own account of his progenitors. It follows from it, that the residence of the Israelites in Egypt could not have extended to four hundred and thirty years; and that, in choosing between this and two hundred and fifteen, we must take the smaller number. One cannot, indeed, very plausibly reconcile the genealogy of Moses even with the shorter period.

. Assuming, then, the period of two hundred and fifteen years, we may calculate the probable increase of two hundred individuals during this time. It must be under favourable circumstances that they would, through such a period, double their numbers once in twenty-five years. But the Israelites were, according to the account in Exodus, placed in circumstances very unfavourable to their increase during the last eighty years of their residence in Egypt; the king having ordered their male children to be destroyed, and they themselves being reduced to miserable servitude. Supposing them, however, to have been originally two hundred individuals, and to have increased at the rate just mentioned, their numbers, upon leaving Egypt, would have amounted to something less than a hundred thousand, instead of two millions and a half.

But whatever was the rate of increase among the Israelites,

* Exodus vii. 7.   † Genesis xlvi. 11.

no reason can be given why they should have multiplied faster than the Egyptians. That the rate of increase of the former should so vastly exceed that of the latter, as it must have done according to the history in the Pentateuch, is incredible. If the Israelites, at the time of their departure, amounted to two millions and a half, their original number had been increased twelve thousand five hundred times; if it amounted to a hundred thousand, it had been increased five hundred times. But if we suppose merely a million of inhabitants in Egypt at the time when the Israelites entered it, then anything approximating to the lowest rate of increase for the whole population of which they made a part, is obviously out of the question. The writer of the Pentateuch, however, represents a single family of sixty-eight male members as entering one of the principal ancient kingdoms, and in a certain time,—whether two hundred, or four hundred, years, is here unimportant—becoming formidable through their numbers to the other inhabitants of the country, of the population of which it would be unreasonable to suppose that they originally formed a ten-thousandth part.

II. There is much in the history of the Israelites, which becomes incredible on the supposition that their number approached to what it is represented to have been. When, according to the account, the two or three millions of Israelites left Egypt, they were accompanied by " a mixed multitude who went along with them, and flocks and herds, even an abundance of cattle."* Yet this immense body is represented as having been collected, arrayed, and put in motion in a single day, in consequence of a hasty command of Pharaoh given the preceding night.† In what time could

* Exodus xii. 33.
† Exodus xii. Numbers xxxiii. 3. The passover was slain on the fourteenth day of the month, which, according to the Jewish computation, ended at sunset. At midnight, that is, on the fifteenth day, the first-born of the Egyptians were destroyed. The same night Pharaoh issued his order for the departure of the Israelites; and during the fifteenth day the Israelites were on their march. I should not mention these particulars, which are obvious in the passages referred to, had I not observed an oversight in the valuable

this nation of men, women, and children, with all their sick and aged, with their domestic animals, and their necessary baggage, have defiled, in the face of any enemy, through the Red Sea? According to the history, it was done in a single night. How long must it have taken such a multitude of men and cattle to quench the thirst of which they were perishing at the waters of Marah, or by those which gushed from the rock of Horeb? What extent of territory must have been covered by two or three millions of men encamped in tents among the rocky defiles, the mountainous and broken country around Sinai, or along the eastern shore of the Red Sea? From the history we should receive the impression that they were a body capable of being readily assembled, and orally addressed by Moses or Aaron; a body which might all be put in motion in the morning, accomplish a day's journey, and at night encamp at a particular place; as at "Elim, where there were twelve wells of water, and they encamped there by the waters."*

III. The number of the Israelites, we are told, had alarmed one of the kings of Egypt. Before the birth of Moses, that is, about eighty years before the Israelites left Egypt, or one hundred and thirty-five after the family of sixty-eight males entered it, the king is represented as saying: "Lo the people of Israel are more numerous and stronger than we; come, let us wisely prevent their multiplying."† Being alarmed at their numbers, he resolved to provoke their most deadly and desperate hatred. He "made their lives bitter" by reducing them to slavery; and issued

---

* "Biblical Researches" of Professor Robinson, to which he seems to have been unconsciously led by an indistinct sense of the utter incredibility of the narrative as actually given. He says (Vol. i. p. 80), "From the time when Pharaoh dismissed Moses and Aaron in the night of [following] the fourteenth day of the month (according to the Jewish reckoning), until the morning of the fifteenth day, when the people set off, there was an interval of some thirty hours." Between some time after the midnight which followed the fourteenth day of the month, and the morning of the fifteenth, there could have been an interval of but a very few hours.

  * Exodus xv. 27.      † Exodus i. 9, 10.

an order for the destruction of all their male children. After an unsuccessful attempt fully to effect his latter purpose, this order is said to have assumed the following horrible form: "Then Pharaoh charged all his people, saying, Every son that is born ye shall cast into the river."* To outrage to the utmost a formidable nation, to exercise upon it an extravagance of cruelty which no tribe of men, however feeble, would tamely endure, virtually to declare a war of extermination upon the Israelites, in the most odious form which war could assume, are the expedients that Pharaoh is represented as adopting through dread of their enmity. Nor is this the most extraordinary part of the history. The Israelites, as far as appears from it, submitted without resistance to be made slaves, and to have their infants murdered as a matter of common usage. The voice of human nature pronounces this to be impossible. No people was ever so far degraded below the brutes, who expose their own lives in defence of their young.

IV. But the king is represented as, at the same time, in dread of their power, and fearful lest they should withdraw themselves from Egypt; lest they should join his enemies, and by force of arms leave the country;"† and, according to the narrative, one of his successors considered their remaining in Egypt as of so much importance that he manifested the most insane obstinacy in refusing to permit their departure. It must have been only for their value as slaves that the kings of Egypt were so desirous to keep the Hebrews in their land. But how is this to be reconciled with an order for the destruction of their male children—that is, for the gradual extermination of those Hebrew slaves, who were such valuable property that supernatural inflictions of the most terrible kind were to be endured, or the hazard of them encountered, rather than that they should be suffered to quit the country?

\* Exodus i. 22. † Exodus i. 10.

V. When at last an order for their departure was extorted, we find them represented as leaving the country in such haste that they "took their unleavened dough in their kneading vessels, wrapped up in their garments, upon their shoulders;" and during their first day's journey "baked unleavened cakes of the dough;" "for they were thrust out of Egypt, and could not tarry; nor had they prepared for themselves any provision."\* As we have before remarked, however, they carried with them "flocks and herds, even an abundance of cattle;" and they carried them into the desert which borders the Red Sea to the west, where no supply of herbage was to be found for their subsistence. Crossing the Red Sea, they commenced their march toward Mount Sinai, through a region of frightful sterility. In this desert they journeyed for three days without water, and, as would appear from the preceding account, without food. At the end of the third day they were furnished with sweet water by a miracle.† What number had perished in the mean time is not told. During their whole journeying and residence along the coast of the Red Sea and in the desert of Sinai, where water for a few travellers is often difficult to be procured, we read of their having a miraculous supply only in one other instance.‡ Their sufferings from hunger, we are told, were great before their arrival at Sinai; and quails and manna were miraculously provided for their support.§ Their cattle, of course, had perished, or been killed. The manna was continued for the whole forty years of their journeyings till they came "to an inhabited land." Yet before quitting their encampment around Sinai, they are again described as having an abundance of cattle for sacrifices, and of lambs for the passover, flour, oil, and wine, and a profusion of spices.‖ Departing from Mount Sinai to march through "a great and terrible

---

\* Exodus xii. 34, 39.  † Exod. xv. 22-25.
‡ At Horeb. Exod. xvii. 1, seqq.  § Exod. xvi.
‖ Exod. Ch. xxiv. 5. Ch. xxix. Ch. xxx. 23, seqq. Leviticus, Ch. viii. ix. Numbers, Ch. iii. 41, 45. Ch. vii. Ch. ix. 2-14, &c.

wilderness,"\* the people complained and wept, saying, " Who will give us flesh to eat ;" and were again miraculously supplied with quails.† After this, their sufferings from want of water return; but their cattle are still alive; for they thus expostulate with Moses and Aaron: " Why have ye brought the people of God into this wilderness, where both ourselves and our cattle must die ?"‡ Thus the whole nation of the Israelites, and not these only, but "a mixed multitude who went with them,"§ are represented as remaining forty years in deserts, where they must have perished but for a constant miraculous supply of food; and as having at the same time herds of cattle, which, in their longings after flesh, they refrained from eating. The food of their cattle must also have been furnished by some astonishing miracle, of which the historian has supplied no account. Equally for men and beasts an uninterrupted miraculous supply of water was necessary; but the supposition that such an uninterrupted supply was afforded, is precluded by the circumstance that four particular cases are specified in which it was given."‖ The Jewish Rabbis, though in general not apt to startle at absurdities, perceived this deficiency in their history, and endeavoured to supply it by a tradition, alluded to by St. Paul,¶ that the rock of Horeb, or the water which gushed from it, followed the Israelites in their wanderings.

VI. An incongruity, only less glaring, is found in the accounts of the wealth possessed by the Israelites, while encamped around Sinai, in gold, silver, brass, precious stones, fine linen of different colours, boards of setim wood, aromatics, spices, and various other articles of luxury, and of their skill in different arts.\*\* They could have acquired

---

\* Deut. i. 19. † Numbers, Ch. xi.
‡ Numbers xx. 4. § Exod. xii. 38. Numbers xi. 4.
‖ At Marah, Exod. xv. 23, seqq. At Horeb, Exod. xvii. 1, seqq. At Meribah, Numbers xx. 2, seqq. And at Beer, Numbers xxi. 16, seqq.
¶ 1 Corinthians x. 4. On which passage see Wetstein's note.
\*\* Exod. Ch. xxv. xxviii. Ch. xxx.-xxxi. Ch. xxxii. 2-4, 20, 24. Ch. xxxv.-xxxix.

neither their wealth nor their skill by their employment as slaves in Egypt in the making of bricks.\* Their skill, it may be said, was miraculously conferred. But this solution will not apply to the casting of the golden calf by Aaron.† A part of their wealth, it may be said, that they procured from the Egyptians, from whom, before leaving Egypt, they asked and obtained " utensils of silver, utensils of gold, and raiment."‡ The story of " their spoiling of the Egyptians," in consequence of a divine direction, presents difficulties quite as serious as those which it may be brought forward to remove. But, however great may have been the generosity of the Egyptians in gifts of gold and silver utensils and raiment, it will account only for a part of the wealth of the Israelites, much of which consisted in other stores. Nor is any explanation to be given why the Israelites, who were re-

---

\* In speaking of the account of the construction of the tabernacle, Dr. Priestley says ("Notes on Scripture," Exod. xxxvi. 5), "In short, there is no art known to the ancients, a thousand years after this time, with which the Israelites do not appear to have been well acquainted." It is strange, that a man of so much acuteness as Dr. Priestley should have written such a sentence without perceiving its obvious bearing on the credibility of the history. The coincidence between his mention of "a thousand years after the time" of Moses, and the not improbable date of the final compilation of the Pentateuch, is perhaps worthy of notice.—We are told, in the Book of Samuel, that some centuries after the period when the Israelites are represented as so skilful in the arts, "there was no smith in Israel," so that they had neither swords nor spears; and "all the Israelites went down to the Philistines to sharpen every man his share, and his coulter, and his axe, and his mattock." (1 Samuel xiii. 19-22.)

† Exodus xxxii.—The opinion entertained by some commentators, that Aaron carved the image in wood, and then overlaid it with gold, which is thought to lighten the difficulties attending the narrative, seems to be inconsistent with its being called a molten calf, and directly contrary to what Aaron is made to say (v. 24), "Then I cast the gold into the fire, and there came out this calf."

‡ Exodus iii. 21, 22; xi. 2; xii. 35, 36. The common version says, that the Israelites "borrowed" of the Egyptians, and the Egyptians "lent" them what they asked for. If they "borrowed," it was with a promise of returning, expressed or implied. But it is far from certain, that the words in the original correspond to those terms, the use of which I have, therefore, avoided. The one party asked as presents, it has been said, and the other party gave, gold and silver utensils (not jewels), and raiment. The causes which have been assigned for this extraordinary liberality of the Egyptians are such, it seems to me, as will bear no discussion.

moving such a profusion of articles of luxury into the desert, and who consequently had provided means for the conveyance of them, should have borne away in the hurry of their departure their yet unleavened dough in the kneading-vessels upon their shoulders, and should have had no opportunity to provide any store of provisions for their own sustenance. If the Israelites possessed all those articles in the desert, they had, as I have said, means of transporting them. But such does not appear to have been the case. The camel is the only beast of burden which could have been used; and there is no mention of their possessing camels.

VII. Concerning the inhabitants of Palestine, the Israelites are said to have been told by Moses, "Ye may not destroy them at once, lest the wild beasts increase upon you." They were, therefore, to be expelled " by little and little," in proportion to the gradual increase of the Hebrews.* These nations, however, would not have waited in peace to be extirpated at the convenience of their enemies; and, if engaged with them in a war of extermination, they would have been more formidable than the wild beasts. The mention of the latter is another strange circumstance. Palestine, at the time when it was invaded by the Hebrews, is described as being inhabited by nations greater and more powerful than they (though their numbers had caused fear to the Egyptians), as having in it large cities " walled up to heaven," and as being highly cultivated, " flowing with milk and honey."†
The whole extent of Palestine is less than two hundred miles in length, and a hundred in average breadth. Supposing the Israelites to have been the sole inhabitants of so small a territory, lately so populous, it would not have required that their number should be two millions and a half, nor more than a tenth part of two millions and a half, to secure them from the ravages of wild beasts.

The history contained in the Pentateuch is not to be

* Deut. vii. 22. Exod. xxiii. 29, 30.
† Exod. iii. 8. Numbers xiii. 27, 28. Deut. viii. 7-9; ix. 1, &c.

judged of only by the few examples of apparent impossibilities, or inconsistencies, which I have specified,—not selected, except, indeed, with reference to their being such as might be rendered obvious in a few words. The attempts to explain the Pentateuch as authentic history present a constant struggle with difficulties. The commentator is continually called upon to soften down the features of what seems incredible, and to create hypotheses by which he may reduce what looks like a fabulous tradition from a remote age to a form that may appear consistent with the character of God, the nature of man, and the circumstances of the individuals who are brought into view. As regards this sort of explanation, it is to be remarked, that we may sometimes admit a conjecture possible, though not in itself probable, to explain a difficulty in a history of established credit; but that a history cannot be trustworthy which demands a constant succession of such conjectures.

Before speaking of the narratives of supernatural events, there is one general characteristic of the history, its representation of the conduct and character of the Israelites, too important to be wholly passed over. It must strike every attentive reader, that he is conversant throughout with men whose characters he cannot enter into, whose states of mind he cannot comprehend, who are continually acting in a manner different from that in which he himself would act; men with whom he has nothing in common. The history is inconsistent with human nature. We may take, as an example, the conduct ascribed throughout to the Israelites in relation to the Deity. According to the history, they witnessed, for a long succession of years, displays of miraculous power, the most astonishing, the most magnificent, and the most appalling; a power never suspending its operations, but continually displaying itself in the pillar of cloud, and pillar of flame, in visible descents of the Deity, and even in the supply of their daily food. It was announced to them, that they were selected as the peculiar objects of the favour and protection of the Being whose power was thus made known. Great blessings were promised as the reward of obedience, and terrible punishments threatened for disobedience. Under these circumstances the minds of any human beings must have been wholly subdued. Every motive, from the highest to the lowest; duty, gratitude, hope, fear, pride, in their wonderful distinction; all good in prospect on the one side, and nothing but destruction on the other; and above all, the visible presence of the Almighty, must have determined them to obedience. Yet the conduct of the Israelites is described to have been such, as to justify the language which Moses is said to have addressed to them a little before his death; "From the day in which ye departed from the land of Egypt, until your arrival at this place, ye have been rebelling against Jehovah."*

Let us now attend to the miraculous part of the history, the manner in which God is described as making Himself known to his creatures by acts and words. In some of the conceptions which the Pentateuch presents of the Infinite Being, we perceive, I think, very striking remains of the revelation by Moses, and, as we may reasonably believe, of earlier communications of God to men. The account, for instance, of the Creation, contained in the first chapter of Genesis, appears a monument of magnificent simplicity, when compared with other ancient cosmogonies. The genius of Plato, as displayed in his Timæus, shrinks before it. Throughout the Pentateuch are enforced in the strongest manner the fundamental truths of one Supreme Being, who is God alone, of his interest in the concerns of men, and of his moral government. The latter conception, indeed, is obscured by the imperfect notions of morality belonging to the rude ages, during which the traditions now found in the Pentateuch may be supposed to have been moulded into their present form. The idea of the unmingled benevolence of the Deity, that God is Love, that afflictions and punishments flow from his mercy equally with our joys, is not to be found there; but it is an idea to which the human intellect,

* Deut. ix. 7.

through the aid of revelation, has attained only in its fullest development. But when we compare the conceptions of God presented in the Pentateuch with the representations of heathen divinities in the poems of Homer, we shall perceive the immeasurable superiority of the former. In the great precepts, "Thou shalt love the Lord thy God with all thy heart," and "Thou shalt love thy neighbour as thyself," we find a conception of the foundations of religion and morality, unknown to heathen antiquity. In coming to the Pentateuch we have entered the precincts of true religion, though grotesque shapes are around us, and the heavens are obscured by clouds from which the thunder is rolling.

These remarks respecting the Pentateuch will not appear incongruous with those that follow, if we recollect that its books admit of being viewed in relation to two wholly different standards. If we regard them as a traditionary, erroneous, account of the early revelations of God to men, especially of his revelation through Moses, we may compare their representations of the Deity with the contemporary superstition and idolatry of the heathen world. If we regard them as the work of Moses, and consequently as containing an authentic record of the revelation of God through him, we must compare those representations with the conceptions of God which Christianity has enabled us to form. Such is the comparison now to be instituted, in pursuing the inquiry whether the books of the Pentateuch were written by Moses.

It is not necessary to dwell on the narratives in Genesis concerning the appearances and acts of God. They evidently imply very rude conceptions of his nature. But there is little doubt among those who have examined the subject, that the Book of Genesis is a compilation of prior accounts, oral or written; and it may be said, that the narratives which it contains had gradually assumed their present form, and that Moses thought it best to retain conceptions and language with which his contemporaries were familiar. But it is to be observed, that when we come to the narrative

of facts, of which, if we regard Moses as the author of the
Pentateuch, he had personal experience, the character of the
history does not improve. There is nothing more strange in
the book of Genesis than the narrative in the fourth chapter
of Exodus, in which it is related, that after Moses had been
solemnly commissioned and sent by God to the Israelites,
while "he was on his way, at a lodging-place, Jehovah met
him and sought to slay him,"—with all that follows.
Respecting this branch of our subject, like the former, it
will be necessary to remark particularly only on a few passages, which may serve as representatives of many others.
 I. In the twenty-fourth chapter of Exodus, there is the
following account. "And Jehovah said to Moses, Come up
unto me, thou, and Aaron, Nadab, and Abihu, and seventy of
the elders of Israel, and worship afar off. . . . Then went up
Moses, and Aaron, Nadab, and Abihu, and seventy of the
elders of Israel; and they saw the God of Israel. And
there was under his feet a pavement of lucid sapphire, clear
as the very heavens. And on the chief men of the children
of Israel He laid not his hand; and they saw God; and
they ate and drank. And Jehovah said to Moses, Come up
to me upon the mount, and there remain, and I will give you
tables of stone, with the law and commandments which I
have written, that thou mayst teach the people. . . . And
the glory of Jehovah abode on Mount Sinai, and a cloud
covered it for six days; and the seventh day he called to
Moses from the midst of the cloud. And the sight of the
glory of Jehovah was like a devouring fire on the top of the
mountain in the view of the children of Israel. And Moses
entered into the midst of the cloud and ascended the mountain. And Moses was upon the mountain forty days and
forty nights. And Jehovah spake to Moses, saying"—
 Before proceeding further, let us consider, that according
to the history, we are about to listen, as it were, to the very
words of God, addressed to that minister with whom He
" spoke as man to man." After all this tremendous solemnity
of preparation, after having been summoned into the visible
presence of the Deity, after having seen God and lived, what

must have been the expectation of the elders of Israel respecting the momentous import of the divine communication? Let us imagine that some of their number had formed just and enlarged conceptions of God, and had speculated upon the condition and prospects of mankind. They must have been looking earnestly for some revelation, which would send a stream of light through the darkness that rested upon the world; which would disclose to their erring and suffering race new relations and new hopes; which should raise man in his moral nature nearer to the author of his being; which should be listened to with intense interest, wherever made known, by all human beings in all ages to come. What, then, was the communication?

"And Jehovah spake to Moses, saying; Tell the children of Israel to bring me an offering. From every one whose heart is willing to give ye shall take my offering. And these are the offerings which ye shall take from them; gold, and silver, and brass, and blue, and purple, and scarlet, and fine linen, and goats' hair, and rams' skins dyed red, and seals' skins, and setim wood, oil for the lamps, aromatics for the anointing oil and for the sweet incense; onyx stones and other stones, to be set in the ephod and breastplate. And let them make me a sanctuary, that I may dwell among them. Ye shall make it according to the pattern of the tabernacle, and all its utensils, which I show thee.

"They shall make an ark of setim wood, two cubits and a half in length, and a cubit and a half in breadth, and a cubit and a half in height; and thou shalt overlay it with pure gold. Within and without shalt thou overlay it; and thou shalt make a moulding of gold about it."

We may stop here; but seven chapters are filled with directions as trivial. So wholly unconnected are they with any moral or religious sentiment, or any truth important or unimportant,—except the melancholy fact of their having been regarded as a divine communication,—that it requires a strong effort to read through with attention these pretended words of the Infinite Being. The natural tendency of a belief that such words proceeded from Him, whenever this belief prevailed, must have been to draw away the regard of the Jews from all that is worthy of man as a moral and intellectual being, and to fix it on the humblest objects of superstition. It is not to be forgotten, however, that this tendency was strongly counteracted by much of a different character that is to be found in the Pentateuch.

II. But throughout the Pentateuch such accounts of the Supreme Being occur, as may excuse or justify the unfavourable conceptions entertained by the Gnostics of the God of the Jews. It is related, for instance, that He inflicted the most terrible evils upon the Egyptians, solely on account of the mad obstinacy of their despot, from whose tyranny they without doubt were already suffering in common with the Israelites.* But passing over every other, less striking, example of the same kind, we will advert only to the order for the extirpation of the Canaanites; and to the manner in which the Midianitish captives are said to have been treated by the command of Moses, acting as the minister of Jehovah.

The expedition sent against the Midianites, after destroying all the adult males, without the loss, as the history relates, of an individual on the part of the Israelites, brought back the women and children as captives. The history thus proceeds: "And Moses was wroth with the commanders of the host . . . . and said, Why have ye saved all the women alive? Lo! they, by the counsel of Balaam, caused the children of Israel to offend Jehovah in the business of Peor, so that there was a plague among the people of Jehovah. Now, therefore, kill every male among the little ones, and every female not a virgin; but the female children that are virgins keep for yourselves."†

If we receive the Pentateuch as authentic, the lot of the female children, who were permitted, certainly not in mercy,

---

* It is not necessary to dwell on the narrative of the "ten plagues of Egypt." Little more, perhaps, can be said than what appears at first sight, to show its improbability; and as little, it seems to me, to remove or palliate this improbability.

† Numbers, Ch. xxxi.

to survive the butchery of their mothers, and of every male among the little ones,—the lot, I say, of these female captives may be judged of by the manners of the times, by the habits which the perpetration of such acts must have produced in the Israelites, by the law respecting female slaves, given in Deuteronomy,* and by the little probability, that even the conditions of this law would be respected.†

The command for the destruction of the Canaanites is expressed in the following words, remarkable for their comprehensive brevity : " Of the cities of these people thou shalt save nothing alive that breathes."‡ Of the objections to the credibility of the Pentateuch, theologians seem to have particularly selected for answer this command, and to have laboured to show, that it is reconcilable with the character of God. It is said, that the destruction of the Canaanites is analogous to those cases in which God appoints a city to be swallowed up by an earthquake, or a nation to be ravaged by a pestilence, without distinction of sex or age. Undoubtedly, the law of nature, that is, the

---

\* Ch. xxi. 10, seqq.

† Bishop Watson, however, in his "Apology for the Bible" (Letter III.), says; "I see nothing in this proceeding but good policy combined with mercy." This remark is followed by some ill-advised declamation. The coarse writer (Paine), against whom he professes to argue, had said, that the Midianitish virgins "were consigned to debauchery by the order of Moses." "Prove this," says the Bishop, "and I will allow that the Bible is what you call it, —a book of lies, wickedness, and blasphemy." The promised concession is equally liberal and injudicious. As a matter of fair statement, the word "debauchery" is objectionable, from its association with modern manners and sentiments. But, if we receive the Pentateuch as authentic, the difference between the actual lot of the Midianitish virgins, and what it is represented to have been by the use of that word, is very narrow and unsafe ground on which to peril the whole credibility of revealed religion.

It may be said in defence of the Jews, that their conduct toward the Midianites was not more barbarous than that of other ancient nations in their wars with each other. This defence might be admitted, if the massacre, according to the account, had not been perpetrated by the express order of Moses, in opposition to the more humane purpose of the army and its leaders. As the case now stands, this apology implies the proposition, that Moses was commissioned by God to sanction and perpetuate the barbarism of his age.

‡ Deut. xx. 16.

merciful law of God, that all must die, takes effect daily upon many thousands of individuals, old men, women, and infants, as well as those able for war. But this obvious truth does not serve to reconcile us to the present account. The ordinary operations of God's providence are not to be confounded with what is represented to have been a miraculous infliction of his vengeance. According to the history, the extirpation of the Canaanites was a terrible punishment from God for their abominable vices and idolatry; but no account can be given why the Deity should manifest Himself to his creatures as inflicting punishment indiscriminately on the innocent and guilty; as an Oriental despot exterminates a family for the offences of its head. But there is more than this to be considered.

The destruction of the Canaanites is to be regarded not merely as the act of God, if ordered by Him, but likewise as the act of those who were the appointed instruments of his will, the chosen people, the sole depositaries of true religion and morals. It is said, that the object of their being appointed the executioners of the decree, was to impress them with the deepest horror of the idolatry and vices of the Canaanites. It is difficult to believe, that any one can give this answer without a strong suspicion of its unsoundness. The effect of their appointment as executioners must have been to convert them into a horde of ferocious and brutal barbarians. It cannot be imagined, that they would have any feelings connected with the performance of a moral or religious duty in the massacre of enemies, between whom and themselves there existed the utmost hatred, that could be produced by a war of extermination; a war which must have seemed to the Canaanites wholly unprovoked and unjustifiable. There is no good moral discipline in the butchery of women and infants. It is not thus that men are to be formed to the service of God. The origin of the supposed direction on which we have been remarking is to be found in the traditionary enmity of the Jews to the Canaanites, and to the ferocity of ancient warfare. The

Jews, sharing in the barbarism of the world, reflected back their own character upon Moses and upon God.

III. I will not enter into the detail of the various precepts and laws, moral, ceremonial, and civil, which are blended together in the Pentateuch without arrangement and with much repetition. Concerning many of them it is incredible that they should have proceeded from the Deity. It is painful and disgusting to associate the distinguishing rite of the Jews with the idea of its having been solemnly appointed by God, and of its having been enforced in the manner related in the story respecting the circumcision of the sons of Moses.* Nothing can render it probable that a law proceeded from God, according to which a man who murdered his male or female slave by beating was to escape with impunity, if the slave did not die under his hands, but survived for a day or two,—with the reason given for it: "For the slave was his property."† Can any

---

\* Exodus iv. 24-26.

† Exodus xxi. 20, 21.—But with this law of the Jewish people may be compared that which Plato gives in relation to the same subject in his imaginary scheme of a perfect code of laws. "Should any man kill a slave, if it be his own, let him purify himself.' (De Legibus, Lib. ix. p. 868.) The master was to be subject to no punishment if he performed a religious expiation. Other laws follow respecting slaves, proposed by Plato, which are shocking to humanity.

The Levitical Law, like the whole Pentateuch, is to be viewed under two aspects. It is to be regarded, on the one hand, in reference to such a code as might, in our apprehension, be worthy of God ; and, on the other hand, it is to be compared with such laws, and such conceptions of justice, as actually existed among heathen nations. When thus compared, there are in the laws respecting persons and property, what may seem clear traces of the effects of that divine dispensation which the Jews had enjoyed, appearing in a higher sense of justice and humanity. The laws respecting slaves, generally, notwithstanding that above quoted, provided for their security and welfare in a manner unknown among the Greeks or Romans. Among the Romans, till the time of the Emperors, a master had absolute power over his slave, unchecked, or rather unnoticed, by any law, so that he might put him to death by torture; and this power, as we may readily believe, was sometimes horribly abused. Nor does the condition of slaves in Greece appear, in general, to have been less unhappy. How they were regarded at Athens may be judged of by the laws proposed by Plato. [*See note* D *at the end of the volume.*—ED.]

one, at the present day, persuade himself, that he is to refer to the Deity laws such as the following? "A man or a woman who has a familiar spirit, or is a divine, shall surely be put to death;"* "Thou shalt not suffer a witch to live;" †—laws, which have been the main support of one of the most debasing and cruel superstitions by which the Christian world has been disgraced. We have seen that there is, properly speaking, no historical evidence for the genuineness of the Pentateuch. What, it may be asked, is the amount of evidence, which would render the question worth discussing? Whether it be true or not, that " the Lord spoke to Moses and Aaron, saying, . . . . Of birds ye shall have these in abomination; they are not to be eaten, they are an abomination, the eagle, the vulture, the osprey; the falcon, kites of every kind, ravens of every kind," &c.; or that these and other similar injunctions should have been thus enforced: "Ye shall not make yourselves abominable by eating any creeping reptile, nor make yourselves unclean and defiled thereby. For I Jehovah am your God. Ye shall therefore sanctify yourselves, and ye shall be holy, for I am holy."‡ To teach men, in the most solemn manner, that to refrain from particular kinds of food is essential to holiness, must tend only to pervert all their conceptions of holiness, duty, and God. The prohibition becomes more strange when we find articles of food enumerated to which nothing but the extremity of hunger could induce men to have recourse. It is unnecessary to observe

---

\* Leviticus xx. 27.
† Exodus xxii. 18. See also Deuteronomy xviii. 9-12.—It has been contended by some in modern times, that these laws do not sanction the belief in witchcraft, but were directed only against impostors, falsely pretending to magical powers. But if such individuals had been meant, they would have been designated according to their true character as impostors, not in language which conveyed the idea, as plainly as any language could do, that their pretences were well founded. The belief in magic appears to have been universal in the ancient world. Such laws as we find in the Pentateuch had their origin in this belief, and could not be understood but as confirming it.
‡ Leviticus xi.

that there are many of the Jewish laws on which delicacy forbids one to comment.*

The general aspect of the Jewish religion, as it appears in the books of the Pentateuch, may lead to the conclusion, that at the time of the compilation of those books, the original doctrine of Moses had been greatly corrupted. The multiplication of trifling and burdensome ceremonies has been in every other case the result of low and very false notions of religion. The observance of such rites has been made a substitute for moral goodness, and in proportion as they have been considered as important in the view of God, has the regard of men being withdrawn from all that constitutes real worth. The state in which our Saviour found the religion of the Jews, upon his appearance on earth, seems a natural consequence of the belief that the Levitical Law had been ordained by God; while, on the other hand, the tendency to such a state may be supposed to have done much gradually to produce and strengthen this belief. We may, perhaps, compare those representations of Christianity which were given during the darkest period of the Romish superstition with that which the Pentateuch affords of the religion of Moses. The existence of the Gospels alone prevented the history of Christ from becoming equally fabulous with that of the Jewish prophet. Some of the apocryphal gospels, as those of the Infancy (as they are called), show the strong tendency to this result.

* No considerations of this kind, however, restrained the learned Michaelis from discussing them at length. Of his "Commentaries on the Laws of Moses," originally delivered in Lectures to his pupils at Göttingen, it is not speaking too harshly to say, that its most striking characteristics are silliness and obscenity. Of the proper application of the latter term there can be no doubt; as to the former, I know of none beside so well suited to express the frivolous gossip, and the wretched attempts at reasoning, with which the work abounds. The historian Müller says of Michaelis, whose lectures he attended when a young man, that he was "homme d'esprit d'ailleurs et très savant; mais qui par sa manière burlesque de traduire et de commenter les poëmes des sages et des inspirés du peuple hébreu, en rendit pour quelque temps la lecture insoutenable à son disciple." (Lettres de Jean de Müller, précédées de sa Vie, p. xv.) Without doubt, such instructors were one cause of the deplorable state of religious speculation that has in our day existed in Germany.

The views just given respecting the Levitical Law, are confirmed by much that is found in the Pentateuch itself, and in other books of the Old Testament; but especially by the representations given in some of the Psalms, and in the earlier prophetical books. The authors of those writings insist in the strongest terms on moral goodness as the recommendation to God's favour, and dwell on the worthlessness of ritual observances. They use language which is apparently irreconcilable with the supposition, that they recognized the Levitical Law as appointed by God, or the history contained in the Pentateuch as authentic. To this subject we will next attend.

## SECTION VI.

ON THE VIEWS OF RELIGION PRESENTED IN THE WRITINGS OF THE JEWISH PROPHETS, AND IN THE PSALMS, COMPARED WITH THOSE FOUND IN THE PENTATEUCH.

IT has been remarked, as affording evidence that the Pentateuch was not the work of Moses, that its authority is not appealed to by the Jewish prophets, the public teachers of religion among the Jews. But the writings of the higher class of prophets furnish evidence more direct to establish the same conclusion.

The religion inculcated in the Pentateuch consists very much in rites, and especially in offerings and sacrifices. The precepts concerning rites are multiplied, reiterated, and enforced in the most solemn manner. But by the prophets *before the Captivity*, such observances are spoken of in the most disparaging terms. The language in which our Saviour has been supposed to have *repealed* the Levitical Law is not more full and explicit. But those prophets had no authority to repeal that Law. Their language, therefore, proves that they did not recognize such observances as enforced by God, and, consequently, that they knew nothing of the Pentateuch as the work of Moses. Their spirit is wholly different from that which appears in the Levitical Law. They insist in the strongest terms upon moral goodness as the sole recommendation to God's favour.

But it may be said, that the prophets are to be understood as disparaging the observance of the ceremonial Law, only when such observance was made a substitute for higher duties, or was practised by habitual transgressors; and were, therefore, far from teaching that a strict regard to its rites, as ordained by God, was not in the highest degree obligatory. This may appear at first view a plausible explanation of much of their language. But it is to be recollected, that if the Law proceeded from God, then the observance of the rites of the Law was a most solemn duty, taking its rank, so far as the Jews were concerned, with the clearest of those obligations, which are imperative upon all men. The explanation given, therefore, supposes that the prophets spoke contemptuously of one duty in order to excite men to perform other duties; that they treated with disrespect what God had commanded in order to lead men to obey his will. On the supposition, that the Levitical Law was ordained by God, the Jews offered sacrifices, and observed the other rites of that Law, because they believed them to have been commanded by God, and with the view of obtaining his favour. Thus far they acted right; and they were not to be reproved and discouraged in doing right, whatever, on the other hand, might be their deficiencies and sins. But, further than this, if there were no intrinsic moral worth in the ceremonies of the Law, then they could have been ordained only as means of holiness; and the absence of holiness in the people afforded no reason for repelling them from the appointed means of obtaining it. According to the representations of the Jewish history, they could hardly, at any time, have been a more perverse and disobedient race than their ancestors on whom those ceremonies were enjoined. It would, therefore, seem, that those who have acquiesced in the explanation that has been mentioned, can have done so only through unconsciously transferring to the prophets their own secret and unacknowledged sense, unacknowledged even to themselves, of the worthlessness of the rites of the Levitical Law. The observance of them, it is agreed, did not constitute holiness; nor can it appear a suitable means of attaining it, if, as the explanation supposes, actual holiness was necessary to render such observance anything but a matter of reprehension.

To illustrate the subject, let us imagine that the practices at one time in high repute in the Romish Church, fasting, the scourging of one's self, other self-inflicted sufferings, and the iteration of forms of prayer, all which were supposed to be conformable to the will of God, had been in fact expressly and most solemnly enjoined by Him. It is evident, that no preacher of true religion, under a conviction that such was the fact, could, by way of reforming the Roman Catholic Church, even when fallen into its most corrupt state, have spoken of those practices contemptuously, or have made a disparaging comparison of them with other duties which he was recommending, or have ventured, through any licence of rhetorical language, to represent them as not ordained and not required by God. The application of this imaginary case to the real case before us is too obvious to be dwelt upon.

With these general views let us consider some of the passages that occur in the writings of the prophets and in the Psalms.

The prophet Amos ascribes these words to Jehovah.*
" I hate, I despise your feasts;
I have no delight in your solemn assemblies;
When ye offer me burnt-offerings and flour-offerings,
   I will not accept them;
Nor will I look on the peace-offerings of your fatlings.
Away with the noise of your songs:
I will not listen to your harping:
But let justice flow as water,
And righteousness like a mighty river.
Did ye offer me sacrifices and offerings
   In the wilderness, for forty years, O house of Israel?"

* Ch. v. 21-25.

Besides the general character of this passage, the concluding question may be particularly remarked. It is equivalent to a strong affirmation, that the Israelites did not offer sacrifices and offerings during the forty years after their leaving Egypt. But this is directly contrary to what is related in the Pentateuch.

Nothing can be more striking than the following passage from Micah.*

" ' With what shall I appear before Jehovah,
And bow myself before the Most High God?
Shall I come before him with burnt-offerings,
With calves of a year old?
Will Jehovah be pleased with thousands of rams;
Or ten thousand of rivers of oil?
Shall I give my first-born for my transgression;
The fruit of my body for my sin?'
' O man! he has made known to thee what is good:
And what does Jehovah require of thee,
But to do justly, and to love mercy,
And to walk humbly before thy God?'"

I pass to the prophet Isaiah.†

" Of what value are the multitude of your sacrifices to me? says Jehovah.
I am weary of the burnt-offerings of rams, and the fat of fed beasts;
And I delight not in the blood of bullocks, or of lambs, or of goats.
Who hath required this of you, when ye come to appear before me, to trample my courts?
Bring no more vain oblations."

. . . . .

\* Ch. vi. 6-8 † Ch. i. 11-17.

"Wash you; make you clean;
Put away your evil deeds from before my eyes;
Cease to do evil; learn to do well;
Seek to do justice; relieve the oppressed;
Do right to the fatherless; defend the cause of the widow."

The following passage is from Jeremiah.\* It may be remarked, that it was written after the discovery, as represented, of "the Book of the Law," in the reign of Josiah, and the events immediately consequent.

"Thus says Jehovah, God of hosts, God of Israel:
Put your burnt-offerings with your sacrifices, and eat the flesh;
For I spake not to your fathers,
Nor commanded them, in the day when I brought them out of Egypt,
Concerning burnt-offerings and sacrifices.
But this did I command them, saying,
Obey my voice, and I will be your God,
And ye shall be my people."

"I spake not to your fathers, when I brought them out of Egypt, concerning burnt-offerings and sacrifices." With what astonishment must this declaration have been listened to by a contemporary Jew, believing the history in the Pentateuch, and consequently believing that the ceremonial Law was ordained by God. And with what feelings would he have regarded the prophet, if, upon questioning him as to his meaning, he had explained himself, as he has been most plausibly explained by modern commentators, in words like these:—I did not mean to say, that God had "appointed no religious rites, such as sacrifices. For the most particular directions are given concerning them in the books of Moses." But I only intended, that God had "always

---

\* Ch. vii. 21 22.

laid less stress upon everything of this kind than upon moral virtue." *

In the Pentateuch, Jehovah is repeatedly introduced as saying, "I am a jealous God, visiting the iniquity of fathers upon children to the third and fourth generation of them that hate me."† With this declaration may be compared the eighteenth chapter of Ezekiel.

"The word of Jehovah came to me again, saying;
"What mean ye, that ye use this proverb concerning the land of Israel, ''The fathers have eaten sour grapes, and the children's teeth are on edge.'
"As I live, saith the Lord, Jehovah, Ye shall not have occasion any more to use this proverb in Israel."

. . . . .

"The son shall not bear the iniquity of the father, nor shall the father bear the iniquity of the son.
"The righteousness of the righteous shall be upon him, and the wickedness of the wicked shall be upon him."

According to the Talmud, there was a discussion among the ancient Jewish doctors about allowing the book now ascribed to Ezekiel a place in the canon, and the majority were at one time disposed to reject it. Their objections to it were founded, it is said, upon passages contained in it, which were regarded as contradictory to the Pentateuch. ‡

It seems, from the book ascribed to him, that Ezekiel wrote during the Captivity. It is a work which is not to be generally referred to as presenting correct or agreeable representations of religion or of the Supreme Being. It is made repulsive by other characteristics beside its great

---

* The words marked as quoted are taken from Dr. Priestley's note on the passage. I quote him only because he has expressed briefly and distinctly what has been said by many others.

† Exod. xx. 5 ; xxxiv. 7.  Numbers xiv. 18.  Deut. v. 9.

‡ Bartoloccii Biblioth. Hebr. P. ii. pp. 847, 848. Wolfii Biblioth. Hebr. Tom. ii. p. 156.

obscurity. If the last nine chapters were written by him, it would appear that his mind was much occupied about ritual observances. But, putting aside what in these chapters it is difficult or impossible to understand, one striking fact presents itself. It is the want of correspondence between the directions for sacrifices there given and those found in the Pentateuch.*

With such passages as have been adduced from the prophets may be connected the remarkable quotation before given from one of the Psalms.† And there is a special reason for adding to them the declaration ascribed to God by Hosea.‡

" I desire goodness and not sacrifices,
And the knowledge of God rather than burnt offerings."

" Go ye and learn," said our Saviour, " what this means, *I desire goodness and not sacrifices.*"§ By thus adopting and sanctioning the declaration of the prophet, he bore testimony that the true character and spirit of the religion of Moses were not to be found in the ritual Law, but that they were identical, as far as that declaration extends, with the spirit and character of his own. He places the prophet for a moment on a level with himself, as equally with himself rejecting the conception, that ceremonial observances were a means of obtaining God's favour.

Such passages as we have been considering may be thrown into stronger relief by comparing them with what appears in a later writer, who is to be referred to the same general class with those from whom we have quoted. Malachi was the last of the prophets, or, in other words, the last of those public religious teachers among the Jews to whom that name has been given. He lived, as is commonly thought, about a century after the return of the Jews to

---

* Compare, for example, the forty-fifth and forth-sixth chapters of Ezekiel, with the twenty-eighth and twenty-ninth chapters of Numbers.
† See before, p. 29.  ‡ Ch. vi. 6.  § Matthew ix. 13.

Palestine, that is, about four hundred years before Christ, when the authority of the ceremonial Law was established. His language in relation to it does not correspond with that of the prophets before the Captivity, but by its contrast it brings out in a more striking manner the character of those religious sentiments which they express, and serves to confirm the opinion, that the Levitical Law, in its present form, was not believed to be of divine authority among the Jews till after their return from their Captivity. Nothing answering to such passages as the following is to be found in any writer before that time.

" But ye say, Wherein have we despised thy name?
Ye bring polluted food to my altar.
Yet ye say, Wherein have we polluted thee?
In that ye say, The table of Jehovah is despicable.
For when ye bring blind animals for sacrifice, ye say,
    It is not evil.
And when ye bring lame and sick animals, ye say, It
    is not evil." *

. . . . .

" Ye bring what has been plundered, and what is lame
    and sick,
And present it for an offering.
Shall I accept it from your hands? says Jehovah.
Cursed be the deceiver who has a male in his flock,
And vows and sacrifices to Jehovah what is marred." †

. . . . .

" Shall a man rob God?
Yet ye rob me.
But ye say, In what have we robbed thee?
In tithes and offerings.
Ye are cursed with a curse;
For ye have robbed me, even this whole nation.
Bring ye all the tithes into the storehouse,
And let there be food in my house." ‡

\* Ch. i. 6-8.     † Ch. i. 13, 14.     ‡ Ch. iii. 8-10.

With these representations of the Deity we may compare those of an earlier writer, the author of the fiftieth Psalm.
" I will reprove thee, not for the sake of thy sacrifices,
Nor of thy burnt-offerings, which are daily before me.
I will take no bullock from thy stalls,
Nor he-goat from thy folds;
For all the beasts of the forest are mine,
And the cattle on a thousand hills.
I know all the birds of the mountains;
And the wild beasts of the plains are before me.
If I were hungry, I would not tell thee:
For the world is mine, and all that is therein.
Do I eat the flesh of bulls?
Or drink the blood of goats?
Offer to God thanksgiving;
And fulfil thy vows to the Most High;
Then call upon me in the day of trouble;
And I will deliver thee, and thou shalt glorify me." *

In such passages appears, as I conceive, the true spirit of the religion which Moses was commissioned to teach; and it is remarkable, that this spirit survived the belief that the Levitical Law was ordained by God through him. Religious sentiments, coincident with those which have been

---

* In the next Psalm (the fifty-first), a Psalm expressing deep penitence in the writer, is the following passage:—

"Thou desirest not sacrifice; else would I give it;
Thou dost not delight in burnt-offerings.
The sacrifice which God loves is a broken spirit;
A broken and a contrite heart, O God, thou wilt not despise."

I notice this passage principally to observe, that there seems little doubt, that the two verses which follow it are (as has been supposed) an addition by a later writer, after the Captivity. They not only have no connection with what precedes, but they stand in direct opposition to what has just been said by the original author. The verses referred to are these:—

" Do good to Zion according to thy mercy;
Build up the walls of Jerusalem;
Then shalt thou be pleased with right sacrifices,
With whole burnt-offerings;
Then shall bullocks be offered on thine altar."

quoted from the earlier prophetical writings and the Psalms, are to be found in the higher class of Jewish writers of later times. Thus the author of Ecclesiasticus says: *
"He who keeps the Law"—(a remarkable expression as defining what might be meant by "keeping the Law")— "He who keeps the Law abounds in offerings; he who gives heed to the commandments offers a peace-offering; he who returns a favour makes an offering of fine flour; he who gives alms offers a thank-offering; he who departs from wickedness is accepted by the Lord; and to forsake iniquity is a sin-offering."

If inserted in any part of Leviticus, what a contrast would this passage form to the general tenor of that book! It is remarkable, likewise, as showing what, in the view of the writer, was meant by "keeping the Law;" that is to say, the performance of duties of universal obligation, exclusively of the observance of the ceremonial Law. As appears, however, from the passage itself, the ceremonial Law was fully established in his time; and he accordingly subjoins, "Thou shalt not appear before the Lord with empty hands; for all these things are to be done for the sake of the ordinances."

The philosophical Jews of Alexandria appear to have laid little stress on the literal observance of the ritual Law, regarding all its precepts as symbolical. "God," says Philo, "rejoices in devout affections, in men striving after holiness; from whom He receives, well pleased, cakes, and barley, and the humblest offerings, as of greater worth than the most costly; and should they bring nothing else, yet making an offering of themselves, perfect in goodness, they would make the best offering, while celebrating God, the Benefactor and Preserver, in hymns of thanksgiving,—some uttered," as he goes on to say, "and some unuttered."†

A few words may be added from another passage of Philo: "True gratitude to God is not shown, as many think, in buildings, gifts, and sacrifices,—for not the whole world

---

\* Ch. xxxv. 1-3.
† De Victimas Offerentibus. Opp. ii. 253.

would be a worthy temple to his honour,—but in praises and hymns, not such as are sung with a loud voice, but such as sound forth in harmony from the invisible and most pure mind." ..... " To confer benefits is the proper office of God; to be grateful, that of the creature, who has nothing but gratitude to give in return. For would he render any other gift, he will find that it already belongs to the Maker of All, and not to the being who brings it. Being instructed, therefore, that there is but one thing for us to do in honouring God—to be grateful, about this let us, at all times and everywhere, be solicitous."*

The continuance and the strength of similar sentiments, among a portion of the Jews, are strikingly manifested by the existence of the sect of the Essenes, and the manner in which they were spoken of. They are described by Philo and Josephus as the most conscientious and religious of their countrymen. It may be observed, though it is not to our immediate purpose, that their religion and morality were of an ascetic and monastic character. Their virtues were those which, in other times, have been produced among Christians as the growth of strong principles in a very corrupt state of society; in such a state of society, as may incline those who would attain the religious character to separate themselves from the world, and, in renouncing its pleasures, to neglect many of its duties. But the Essenes, as I have said, were the most virtuous among their countrymen, in the view even of Philo; and this sect, so regarded by him and by Josephus, offered no sacrifices. " They send gifts to the temple," says Josephus, " but offer no sacrifices; their modes of purification being different; and hence, being excluded from the common sanctuary, they offer themselves as a sacrifice."† And he goes on to say, that " they deserve admiration above all those who have cultivated virtue."‡ " Among them," says Philo, " are especially to be found worshippers of God, men who sacrifice no animals, but deem

---

* De Plantatione Noë. Opp. i. 348.
† ..... ἰφ' αὐτῶν τὰς θυσίας ἐπιτέλουσι,
‡ Antiq. Jud. Lib. xviii. c. 1, § 5.

it their duty to sanctify their own minds." * How was it that Philo and Josephus thus celebrated the religious character of men, who, if the Levitical Law proceeded from God, neglected his express commands? Neither has expressed, nor is it probable that either felt, any doubt, that Moses was the author of the Pentateuch, and that the ritual Law proceeded from God. Philo's system of allegorizing might have enabled him to explain away the whole obvious meaning of its commands concerning sacrifices; but he has not done so in his writings. The answer, therefore, it would seem, is partly, at least, to be found in the general fact, that prevalent errors are often acquiesced in, and even, when directly called in question, zealously defended, by individuals who do not attend to their necessary bearing, on whose prevailing habits of thought and feeling they have very little influence, and who hold truths wholly irreconcilable with them.

There are, then, two very different aspects under which the religion of Moses appears. One is that which is presented in the ritual Law; the other is that which is found in portions of the Pentateuch, in the higher class of writers of the Old Testament, who, as we have seen reason to think, lived before the belief prevailed, that the ritual Law came from God, and even in the higher class of Jewish writers of after times. The spirit of the Jewish religion, as represented by them, is coincident with the spirit of the religion of Christ.

The general conclusion seems to be, that the revelation of God through Moses was made at so remote a period, that no contemporary or early history of it remains; though imperishable monuments of it exist in the effects which it produced; and that there was nothing in this communication of God to a peculiar people,—I do not say contrary to the spirit of the religion of Christ, for this it would be absurd to suppose,—but that there was nothing in it, which the great messenger of God to the whole world was called upon or commissioned to abrogate. He came not "to annul the

---

* Quod liber sit quisquis virtuti studet. Opr. ii. 457.

law and the Prophets,"—that is, the true religion of Moses: but " to perfect." There was an opposition between his religion and the contemporary religion of the Jews, that very corrupt religion which had gradually been formed in their nation ; but certainly no opposition between his religion and that of Moses, if, as we believe, Moses was, like him, a messenger from God.

## SECTION VII.
### ON THE INFERENCES RESPECTING THE LEVITICAL LAW AND THE PENTATEUCH, TO BE DRAWN FROM THE TEACHING AND ACTIONS OF OUR SAVIOUR.

THE ritual Law was done away by Christianity; or, in other words, it was not binding upon Jewish Christians. Of the distinguishing rite of the Jews, St. Paul says to the Galatians, " In Jesus Christ," that is, in Christianity, " neither circumcision avails anything, nor uncircumcision, but faith, showing itself by love ;"* and he reiterates the declaration at the very close of the Epistle.—Philo speaks of the law respecting the Jewish Sabbath as " that most holy and awful law." He relates that a governor of Egypt, in his time, had endeavoured to compel the Jews to violate it, thinking that if this could be effected, it would lead them to abandon all their peculiar customs, and neglect all the ordinances of their religion.† St. Paul says, " One man regards one day more than another, another man regards every day alike. Let each be fully satisfied in his own mind. He who regards the day regards it as a servant of the Lord ; and he who regards not the day regards it not as a servant of the Lord."‡ He is speaking of the observance of the Jewish Sabbath, as an ordinance of the Levitical Law.—We have seen how solemnly the distinction was enforced in this Law between clean and unclean food. " I know," says St. Paul, and am satisfied,

---

\* Galatians v. 6.     † De Somniis. Opp. i. 675.
‡ Romans xiv. 5, 6.

as a disciple of Christ, "that there is nothing unclean in itself; but to him who thinks anything unclean it is unclean."* This is but a very small part of the evidence which his Epistles afford, that he did not consider the Levitical Law as binding upon Christians.

What view he himself entertained of its origin, and of the authorship of the Pentateuch, would be an interesting and curious inquiry, but it is foreign from our present purpose. The Apostles, generally, appear to have long held the prevailing opinions of their countrymen respecting the Law, and probably their minds were always more or less affected by them. It was not till many years after the death of our Saviour that they were satisfied, by an express revelation, that the ritual Law was not to be imposed on the Gentile converts. By the great body of Jewish converts it continued to be observed, and its authority to be zealously maintained. St. Paul, it is evident from the New Testament, incurred much odium among the Jewish believers from his assertion of the truth.

But, if the ritual Law were not binding upon Christians, the question arises upon what ground it was abrogated. Was it, as has been represented, solemnly ordained by God through Moses, and as solemnly annulled by God through Christ? Or was it a law of human growth, a system of superstitious observances, opposed in character and spirit to Christianity, and, therefore, a system, the error of which was involved in the truth of our religion?

Had the ritual Law been, as represented in the Pentateuch, promulgated by God, it is evident that the obligation of the Jews to obey that law could not cease till it was explicitly and solemnly repealed by God. But we find nowhere any declaration of our Saviour recognizing its divine origin, and asserting his commission from God to declare it no longer binding. One of two inferences necessarily follows; either that the law remained binding upon his followers from among the Jews, contrary to what is affirmed by St. Paul, and contrary, as we shall see, to what he himself

* Romans xiv. 14.

taught by his actions and words, or that this law did not proceed from God, and, therefore, that no express declaration was necessary to invalidate its authority.

But it may be asked, on the other hand, Why did not our Saviour explicitly declare the fact, if the ritual law was a system of human superstition? The question, in other words, is this: Why did he not outrage to the uttermost the prejudices of those whom he called upon to be his followers? Many errors connected with religion, of more or less importance, were entertained by his hearers, which he did not undertake to correct. All truth could not be communicated to men so unprepared for, or rather so opposed to, the reception of the few great truths which it was his office to communicate. The revelation from God was not given to do the whole work of human reason on all subjects connected with religion. To imagine the possibility of such a revelation, man's nature and condition continuing as they are, is to imagine an absurdity; for it is to suppose a constant miraculous illumination of all individual minds, extending over so wide a sphere of facts and opinions as to embrace all the more important objects of thought. The attention of his hearers was to be fixed on those fundamental principles of religion that immediately concern the essential and eternal interests of man, and which it was the purpose of his ministry to announce on the authority of God. From those principles their minds were not to be distracted to the consideration of minor topics, which, however important, were incomparably less important. Had he undertaken to correct all the wrong opinions of the Jews, more or less connected with religion, a cloud of misrepresentations, misunderstandings, and controversies, would have arisen, obscuring the whole of his teaching. That in order to accomplish the great purpose of his mission, it was necessary for Jesus to refrain from directly opposing many gross errors of his countrymen, is a fact to be constantly kept in view in considering his history. I have elsewhere endeavoured to illustrate it more fully.*

* "Statement of Reasons for not believing the Doctrines of Trinitarians," Appendix, p. 313, scqq.

But it may be further said, that our Saviour not only did not oppose, but that he asserted and sanctioned the belief of the Jews concerning the Pentateuch and the Levitical Law. There are passages, fewer perhaps than is commonly thought, which would support this proposition, supposing that Jesus had been addressing a body of enlightened and unprejudiced men, and that, moreover, we could be assured that his words were reported with verbal accuracy.

The general spirit and meaning of our Saviour's teaching, as recorded in the Gospels, is free from all uncertainty. If we receive it as the teaching of a divine messenger, it leaves no doubt concerning the fundamental truths of religion—the being of God, God's care for men, and man's immortality and moral responsibility. But in the words ascribed to him, we sometimes meet with difficulties, not affecting the clearness with which those truths were taught, but preventing us from readily or certainly ascertaining the precise purport and bearing of what he said in relation to topics incidentally presented.

Among the various causes by which this uncertainty is produced, there is one perfectly obvious and indisputable, though it has been less regarded, perhaps, than any other. It is, that his words are not always given with verbal accuracy by the different historians of his ministry. We need not recur to any reasoning to show that this fact is in the highest degree probable. The cases in which the Evangelists unquestionably intended to report the same words of Jesus, but in which they differ from each other in their reports, render it certain. It follows that there must be passages, where, to determine the exact meaning that was expressed by our Saviour, we cannot take the precise words of some one of the Evangelists as an infallible guide. When we meet with a difficulty that cannot otherwise be fully solved, the consideration that the reporter may have varied the expression used by Jesus, should enter into our explanation.

Now such unintentional errors, more or less affecting the sense, were most likely to occur on subjects concerning which strong prejudices existed among the Jews, that had moulded their forms of language, if they were prejudices that Jesus did not directly oppose. Everyone easily slides into the language of a popular error, or rather we may find it difficult to avoid such language, when not expressly contending against the error. But, on the supposition that the Evangelists had not decidedly renounced the opinions of their countrymen respecting the Pentateuch and the Levitical Law, we cannot doubt that they might unconsciously attribute to Jesus incidental expressions favouring those opinions; that they might have done so in cases where, if his precise words had been compared with their report of them, they would not have recognized any important difference of character or effect between his language and their own.

The unquestionable fact that the words of our Saviour are not always reported with perfect correctness, is to be kept in view in studying the history of his ministry. It will not lead us to reject any declaration ascribed to him, as not founded on what he actually said, or as not, in its *essential* meaning, true; but it may enter as one element into our explanation of certain passages. It is sometimes evident that it must enter into our explanation; for it sometimes appears, from a comparison of the Evangelists with one another, that the report of our Saviour's language, which we find in one of them, is defective, or otherwise incorrect, and therefore, that this report must be explained with reference to the fact, that it is so.

The general principle of explanation just stated deserves consideration, doubtless, in relation to some of the words ascribed to Jesus that have been thought to express or imply his opinions concerning the origin of the Pentateuch and the Levitical Law. It may, as I have said, enter as one element into their explanation. But we may question how far it is necessary to resort to it, considering that another fact is to be attended to. This is, that our Saviour, on some subjects, and on some occasions, adopted the common language of the Jews, founded on their erroneous conceptions, certainly without any design of sanctioning those conceptions. He sometimes did so for the purpose of changing the meaning of the terms by giving them a new application. Thus the Jews, under the name of "the kingdom of Heaven," expected an earthly kingdom, of which the Messiah was to be the monarch: The idea of such a kingdom alone was excited in their minds, when Jesus announced that the kingdom of Heaven was at hand. But he used the term figuratively, in a very different sense, which was to be gradually explained by subsequent events.—Sometimes he used such language for the purpose of rhetorical illustration, which may be drawn either from fact or fable. "When an unclean spirit," he said, "has gone out of a man, it passes through desert places in search of rest."* No intelligent reader will suppose from these words that our Saviour meant to adopt and sanction the then common notion that desert places were frequented by demons.—At other times he is reasoning upon the false conceptions of those whom he addressed, reasoning *ad hominem,* as it is called. "If I cast out demons through Beëlzebub," he said, "through whom do your disciples cast them out?"† There were some of the school of the Pharisees, it appears, who pretended to cast out demons by exorcism, and who, when they succeeded in producing a real or seeming return to sanity in their patients, were thought to have effected a great work. Our Saviour did not mean to imply that these men possessed powers like his own. The object of his question merely was to expose the prejudices and gross injustice of the Pharisees, who believed that their disciples had, in the one particular in question, similar power to that of Christ, and who, in his case and theirs, regarded its exercise so differently. In such reasoning from false conceptions the language of error is necessarily used. The character of such reasoning may be more or less obvious; and when not perfectly obvious, he who does not exercise his understanding, but looks only at the naked words before him, may insist that a speaker or writer means to affirm an error, which, in fact, he introduces into his discourse only to show its inconsistency with some

---

\* Matthew xii. 43.  † Matthew xii. 27.

other error, or as a temporary stepping-stone on the way to truth. And, beside the occasions that have been mentioned, language founded on the mistaken conceptions of the Jews was employed by our Saviour, either for the sake of producing an effect on the imagination and feelings of his hearers, which could not have been produced, or could not have been produced so powerfully, in any other way, or of conveying some truth to their understandings, which they could not have distinctly apprehended, if expressed in any other form. Thus he spoke, for example, of moral evil, under the terrific personification of Satan. In such cases we must, and we may easily, distinguish his essential meaning from the modes of expression in which it is clothed— modes of expression adapted to Jewish conceptions, but not correspondent to our own. Some of the truths taught by Jesus could not but receive an accidental colouring from the medium of the language through which they were conveyed; and we must not confound this accidental colouring with their essential nature.* But this subject admits some further explanation.

Every language is conformed to the conceptions of those who use it, and consists wholly of the signs or expressions of their conceptions. The progress of knowledge makes necessary the enlargement of a language. The discoveries of modern chemistry, for example, have required a new vocabulary, in which they may be preserved and communicated. When, on any subject of wide extent, the conceptions of the generality of men are erroneous, their errors

* The principle involved in the preceding remarks, that in explaining the words of our Lord we should consider to whom they were immediately addressed, is equally implied in the following passage from Tertullian,—a very remarkable one, considering the time when it was written,—though he makes a different application of it: "Omnia quidem dicta Domini omnibus posita sunt; per aures Judæorum ad nos transierunt, sed pleraque in personas directa, non proprietatem admonitionis nobis constituerunt, sed exemplum." —"All the sayings of our Lord are meant for all; they have passed to us through the ears of the Jews; but many of them, being addressed to individuals, are not, for us, literal precepts, but exemplifications of duty."—De Præscript. Hæretic. c. 8, p. 205. Conf. De Fugâ in Persecutione, c. 13, pp. 542, 543.

enter into the structure of their speech; they are embodied in the words which they use. It is often necessary for him who would correct such errors to introduce new terms, or to give new senses, or a new application, to terms already in use. When circumstances do not require, or admit, that those errors should be controverted, the language in which they are incorporated may be used by one fully acquainted with the truth. It may often be employed with propriety and advantage. There are occasions when, by its use, right conceptions and feelings may be produced, which could not be communicated by language more correct. I understand (for it is a subject on which I am incapable of forming an independent opinion) that, at the present day, many of those qualified to judge, reject the theory of the emission of rays from luminous bodies, and regard the sensation of light as produced by the undulations of a luminous æther, as that of sound is caused by undulations of the air. Supposing this theory to be true, and that it should be universally received, the language which has been formed upon the old belief will not soon, if ever, cease to be the language of common life and of poetry. Though, upon the supposition just made, this language implies throughout what is contrary to the truth; yet it is equally well adapted to the expression of all truths that concern the generality of men, as language conformed to the correct theory. It will, at least for a long time, be better adapted to this purpose, as being more intelligible to the unlearned; more conformed to the appearances, if not to the reality, of things. Nor can we, with our present associations, readily believe, that a similar profusion of figures and imagery to that which poetry now borrows from light may be effectively addressed to men's imagination and feelings through the medium of other forms of language than those to which we are accustomed. So also in Chemistry; however requisite the new nomenclature may be for the purposes of science, it is unimportant, except indirectly, as regards the arts or medicine. The old terms might, in many cases, serve equally well for the practical purposes of life. We might continue to call one substance "the Oil of Vitriol," and another "the Sugar of Lead," and, notwithstanding the erroneous ideas suggested by those names, we might talk of them as intelligently, and explain their properties and uses as correctly, as if we denominated them "Sulphuric Acid," and "the Acetate of Lead;" and, in speaking to those familiar only with the former names, no one would hesitate to use them. Truth, then, may be clearly and effectually conveyed in the language of error; that is to say, in terms having their origin in erroneous conceptions, and adapted to the expression of those conceptions.

In the time of our Saviour, the notions of the Jews on many subjects connected with his preaching were false and superstitious. These notions were necessarily ingrained in their forms of speech. A philosophical language, in which they should be avoided, might undoubtedly have been formed by him; and such a language might have been intelligible to the philosophers, if there were any philosophers, among the Jews. But our Saviour preached to the poor, he addressed multitudes, his immediate disciples were fishermen and taxgatherers, and others of no higher intellectual attainments, and he could use only popular language, such language as his hearers would understand and feel. He might, on a certain occasion, have said, I foresee the triumph of my religion over evil, moral and physical; but even had he been partially understood by his hearers, if they had had some notion of what was meant by "evil, moral and physical," and by "The triumph of his religion," the assertion would have passed over their minds as a shadowy abstraction, and left no impression. He did in fact say, with the same meaning, "I saw Satan falling like lightning from Heaven;" and, in so saying, he used imagery which was adapted to their conceptions and feelings. The whole phraseology of the Jews concerning the Pentateuch and the other books of the Old Testament was moulded on their erroneous opinions respecting those books. Our Saviour might have avoided the use of it, and introduced new modes of speech, conformed to the truth. In this case, it is probable that he would have abundantly excited their attention. Such a fundamental change in their religious language would have exposed him to questioning. Pharisees would have come " to try him " on the subject. What would have been the effect, if he had declined to explain himself? What would have been the consequences, if he had explained himself? In the latter case, unless God had seen fit to use other means than He did for establishing truth among men, the whole ministry of Jesus might have been wasted, and he might have died a martyr to an ineffectual attempt to correct the false opinions of his countrymen in relation to the Old Testament and the Levitical Law. What he did do, that is, what the circumstances of his ministry permitted him to do, to manifest his sense of those errors, will appear hereafter.

Essential truths, then, may be clearly and effectually, sometimes most effectually, conveyed in the language of error. It is true, that one writing at the present day on any subject of morals or religion, who may suppose himself to be addressing intelligent and well-informed readers, is bound, as far as possible, to avoid such language, when it may occasion any mistake as to his meaning. It is his duty to express himself with unequivocal distinctness. But such language, in regard to many topics, constituted the popular, or rather the only, language of the Jews; and our Saviour was placed in circumstances altogether different from those of a philosopher of our own times. That he might not distract the attention of his hearers from the great truths which it was the purpose of his mission to make known, that he might not uselessly alarm their prejudices and rouse their passions, he sometimes adopted their common language, though founded on error. We are not hence to consider him as sanctioning their errors. Such language, as used by him, is to be understood as we always understand the language of error when used by one whom we fully believe to comprehend the truth, and to have no purpose but to express it. We view it as an adaptation of his thoughts to the conceptions of those whom he addresses; or as the presentation of ideas, essentially correct, in the only forms in which they have been embodied in language, though these forms may contain an alloy of error. In the teaching of our Saviour it is the essential meaning alone that is to be regarded. The form of expression may be an accident, resulting from temporary and local circumstances, from the character of those whom he immediately addressed, and, especially, from the nature of their conceptions and language.

The facts that have been stated, in connection with those now generally recognized in the interpretation of the New Testament, may serve to explain the passages in which our Saviour has been thought to sanction the common opinions of the Jews respecting the origin of the Levitical Law and the authorship of the Pentateuch. I will notice, for the sake of illustration, one of those passages, perhaps the most remarkable. In the Gospel of John, our Saviour is represented as thus addressing his Jewish hearers: "Had ye believed Moses, ye would have believed me; *for he wrote concerning me;*" that is, "what he wrote concerns me."\*

Here, it may be said, is an express assertion of our Saviour, that "Moses wrote;" and, if we will not raise an idle cavil, grounded on the supposition, that Moses may have written a part, but not the whole, of the Pentateuch, we must admit him to have been its author; and consequently admit that the Levitical Law proceeded from God.

But, on the other hand, it may be remarked, that to affirm that Moses was the author of the Pentateuch is, obviously, not the main purpose of the passage. Its *essential* meaning is, Had ye received with true faith the religion taught by Moses, and had it produced its proper effect on your minds, ye would have received me; for the dispensation by Moses concerned me; it was intended as a preparation for me.

It is, then, to be considered, that, in regard to the *incidental* meaning supposed to be expressed by the passage as it now stands, it rests wholly on a single word. If, instead of the words, "Moses *wrote* concerning me," our

---

\* John v. 46.

Saviour in fact said, "Moses *taught* concerning me," (that is, What Moses taught concerns me,) then the declaration, without any change in its *essential* meaning, would suggest no such inferences as have been drawn from it. In order, therefore, to draw those inferences from it, we should be certain that St. John reported his Master's language with verbal exactness. But it is not likely that he committed it to writing till many years after it was uttered; and it is altogether probable, that if, when he committed it to writing, the question had been proposed to him, whether our Saviour said "Moses wrote," or "Moses taught," or "Moses spoke," he would have been unable to solve the doubt. Nor is it unreasonable to suppose, that of these expressions, all equally suitable to the *main purpose* of Jesus, he might not have remarked that there was reason for preferring one to another. It is to be recollected, that the fact is unquestionable, that the Evangelists did not always report the language of their Master with verbal exactness.

But, supposing that the words before us are the very words of our Saviour, how are we then to regard them? We may regard them as an address *ad hominem*, as an incidental and temporary adoption of the conceptions and language of those to whom he was speaking, in relation to a subject foreign from his immediate purpose. We may understand him as if he had said: Had ye believed Moses, ye would have believed me, for the books which, *as you suppose*, Moses wrote, concern me. If it be asked, how those books concerned our Saviour, the answer is, that all the truths preserved in those books derived from, or relating to, the revelation by Moses, concerned him for whom this dispensation was preparatory. Those books clearly taught, that there was one God, the Creator of all things, ruling over all things, and exercising a moral government over men,—loving righteousness and hating iniquity. The foundation of all true religion was thus laid. He whose character had been formed on the belief of those truths was prepared to receive the truths taught by Jesus. The books preserving the traditions concerning Moses likewise presented in the strongest light the fact, that the Jews had been miraculously separated by God from other nations. The Jews believed, and reasonably believed, that this separation had been made for some great end, yet unaccomplished. They were expecting a new messenger from God to complete the work. This end was to be accomplished by Christ. He was the expected Messenger,—the Messiah. These, I conceive, are the reasons why the books ascribed to Moses concerned him. Whatever mixture of error they might contain, they still preserved the traditions of that earlier dispensation, the main purpose of which was to prepare for his coming.

In the wide field which is to be traversed in this investigation, we are led to take different views of the Pentateuch, but they are all perfectly reconcilable with each other. We must not estimate its value to a pious Jew before the coming of Christ, by the opinion which an enlightened Christian may now form of its authorship and its errors. To have broadly communicated such an opinion to the former, by way of enlightening his mind on the subject of religion, would have implied anything but wisdom in his religious teacher. A pious Jew perhaps resolved its difficulties into allegories, or more commonly, it may be, passed over them without suffering his attention to dwell upon them, as intelligent Christians have done. There are, perhaps, but few men, into whose system of opinions errors do not enter, irreconcilable with truths which they firmly hold, and such as might have a disastrous effect upon their character. But these errors often lie inert in the mind, unregarded, and inoperative on the feelings and conduct. He whose intentions are right has, at least under favourable circumstances, a moral corrective in his heart for his mistakes of speculation; or, in the inconsistency of his opinions, the true may neutralize the effects of the erroneous.

There are still other considerations to be attended to respecting the relation of Christianity to the Levitical Law. This Law consists of two parts. It was both the Ritual and the Civil Law of the Jews. On the one hand, it regulated the ceremonies of their national religion, and, on the other, it was their statute law concerning civil rights, crimes, and punishments. Now in the simple performance of the ceremonies ordained by it there was no moral harm. What it prescribed might be innocently complied with. Accordingly, we find that Jesus sometimes observed its ordinances, as in the celebration of the Passover; and that they were regarded not only by the other Apostles, but occasionally also by St. Paul, when *to the Jews he became as a Jew*. But so far as the Levitical was the civil law of the nation, obedience to it was not merely innocent, it was a duty, binding upon the followers of Christ, equally with the rest of their countrymen. Thus our Saviour says: " The Teachers of the Law and the Pharisees sit on the seat of Moses," that is, they expound and administer the laws of the nation, they exercise an authority similar to that once held by Moses; "Whatever, therefore, they bid you observe, that observe and do:"\* submit to their authority, as ministers of the law, whatever may be their private vices. Thus, too, when reproving the Teachers of the Law and the Pharisees for their affected scrupulosity in paying tithes of mint, anise and cummin, he said to them; "'These ought ye to do, and not to leave the other undone."† It was a right principle, that the law was to be observed even in its minor requirements.

There was, as I have said, no moral harm simply in the observance of the rites of the Jewish religion by one who considered them as matters of indifference. But, on the supposition that these rites were not ordained by God, there can be no question that the tendency of such a system of ceremonies, regarded as an essential part of religion, was to strengthen, more and more, gross misconceptions of religion and of the religious character; and to produce that outward show of sanctity, accompanied with real depravity, which marked the general character of the Pharisees in the time of Christ. When the observance of ceremonies is raised to the same rank with the performance of duties, in the confusion that ensues, the former usually supersedes the latter. Men

---

\* Matthew xxiii. 2, 3. † Matthew xxiii. 23.

find it much easier to satisfy themselves concerning their religious character by doing certain definite acts, that require no struggle with their evil passions, than by aiming at indefinite improvement, which demands constant humility, watchfulness, and self-control.

The ritual Law, as has been before remarked, was not solemnly repealed by our Saviour in the name of God, as if it had been solemnly promulgated by God; it fell before his teaching like a form of human superstition. The contrariety thus manifested between the character and spirit of his religion and the character and spirit of the ritual Law; the manner, in other words, in which this law was done away by Christianity, shows that the common opinion of the Jews respecting its divine origin was not sanctioned by the teaching of our Saviour. But in relation to this subject there is more to be considered.

If Jesus had publicly and explicitly declared the error of the long-cherished belief of the Jews, such a storm of prejudice and passion would have been excited in the great body of the nation, and such confusion and bewilderment of mind would have been produced among those best disposed to listen to him, as would, to all human apprehension, have defeated the purpose of his ministry. It was a truth to be taught indirectly. But he did not leave it to be inferred only from the character of his religion. He gave other intimations of it, sufficiently intelligible. He went to the very limits, within which a divine wisdom restrained him, in bearing his testimony against the error of the Jews; and this testimony, though its whole effect was not understood, was yet so offensive, that it could not be given but at the hazard of his life.

I refer to that language and those actions of our Saviour, which distinctly imply that the Levitical Law was not of divine origin. In the investigation of this evidence an unexplored subject opens upon us.

It will be recollected in what terms Philo, certainly no bigot for the literal observance of the Levitical Law, speaks of the Jewish Sabbath.* "Whoever does any work on the Sabbath shall surely be put to death," is a law repeatedly given in Exodus.† "Ye shall kindle no fire throughout your dwellings on the Sabbath."‡ In Numbers§ we read, that a man was found gathering sticks on the Sabbath; "and the Lord said to Moses; This man shall surely be put to death; the whole congregation shall stone him with stones without the camp." So strict, according to the Levitical Law, was to be the observance of the Sabbath, and so fearful a crime was any breach of the statute represented to be.

But Jesus repeatedly disregarded, or countenanced the disregard of, the law respecting the Sabbath; and he did so at the hazard of his life. But it is not to be imagined, that he thus manifested his disregard for that Law wantonly; or that such hazard was encountered without the purpose of effecting some important end. What, then, could this end be, except to teach indirectly the superstitious character of such observances as the Levitical Law required, and especially of such representations concerning the extreme guilt of neglecting them, as that Law presented? Let us attend to some of the examples.

When, as he was passing through a field of grain on the Sabbath, ‖ his disciples gathered the ears of grain and ate them, and the Pharisees said; "Lo, thy disciples are doing what the Law forbids on the Sabbath," his reply, it is to be observed, did not contradict their assertion. But, for the obvious reasons before given, he could not *directly* tell them that this Law was not from God, and was not binding upon men. What, then, did he say? He first made one of those annunciations of his high character and of the sanctity of his office, which were so necessary to the accomplishment of his ministry. David, their great monarch, the supposed type of the Messiah, had broken the Law, when himself and his companions were hungry; and what David had done

---

\* See before, p. 85. † Ch. xxxi. 14. Ch. xxxv. 2.
‡ Exodus xxxv. 3. § Ch. xv. 32-36.
‖ Matthew xii. 1-8. Mark ii. 23-28. Luke vi. 1-5.

without censure, he might do without censure. The priests performed their work in the temple on the Sabbath notwithstanding the Law ; and those who addressed him were in the presence of "one greater than the temple." In such declarations there is no recognition of the Divine authority of the Law, and still less in what follows. "But, had ye known what this means, *I desire goodness and not sacrifices*, ye would not have condemned the guiltless." These words imply, that such an observance of the Sabbath as the Law enforced in a manner so terrific had not been required by God, and was not acceptable to Him. "For the Sabbath was made for man, and not man for the Sabbath." The general truth involved in this declaration is, that what God requires man to do is for the benefit of man; He demands no slavish observance of mere ceremonies. "So that the Son of Man is master even of the Sabbath:"—So that I, the messenger of God, have a right to dispense with such ceremonies.

Jesus repeatedly performed his miracles on the Sabbath, twice, as is related, in a synagogue.* To meet the offence of the Jews, at his thus breaking the rest of the day, he presented the same essential idea in different forms of expression. "Who among you, that owns a sheep, if it fall into a pit on the Sabbath, will not lay hold of it and lift it out ? Of how much more worth is a man than a sheep ! It is lawful, then, to do good on the Sabbath." If our Saviour had attached any sanctity to the law respecting the ceremonial observance of the Sabbath; if it had not been his express purpose indirectly to show that he did not regard it as of divine origin, he might, and undoubtedly would, have deferred the performance of his miracle till another day. In justification of his conduct, he taught that all good works, even those for the relief of inferior animals, as the taking of a sheep from a pit, or the leading of an ox or an ass to water, might be performed on the Sabbath. The licence which the Pharisees allowed themselves, in regard to the actions specified, precluded any ready reply to this doctrine. But

* Matthew xii. 9-14. Mark iii. 1-6. Luke vi. 6-11. Luke xiii. 10-11.

how much they were outraged by what he did and what he taught, appears from the narrative: "Then the Pharisees went out, and concerted means to destroy him."

Early in his ministry, at Jerusalem, by the pool of Bethesda, he restored to health one who had been a cripple for thirty-eight years, and directed him to rise, take up his bed and walk. This was done on the Sabbath. The Jews, in consequence, pursued Jesus with the purpose of killing him, "because he had done this on the Sabbath."* They were acting in conformity, as doubtless they thought, to the law in Exodus; "Whoever does any work on the Sabbath shall surely be put to death." "After this Jesus would not, for some time, sojourn in Judea, because the Jews sought to kill him." Afterward he went up to Jerusalem, at the Feast of Tabernacles, and referred, in his first public discourse after his arrival, to the danger to which he had exposed himself, by breaking through the ceremonial observance of the Sabbath. "Why do you seek to kill me?" he asked. Why, when ye allow a child to be circumcised on the Sabbath, "are ye angry with me, because I have restored soundness to the whole body of a man on the Sabbath?"†

We cannot doubt, that Jesus meant to convey some very important instruction in actions which form so prominent a part of his ministry. It could not have been for any light purpose, that he thus repeatedly put his life in jeopardy. Supposing the representations relating to the Sabbath contained in the Pentateuch to be correct, our Saviour would not have pursued the course which he did, merely for the sake of correcting the over-scrupulous notions of some of the more bigoted Jews concerning its observance. The end would have been too trifling, and too little connected with any high moral and religious object, to be aimed at by means so hazardous. Nor, supposing those representations of it correct, would it have been easy for the wisest and most liberal-minded of the Jews to draw a line between the scrupulous observance of the day, which was so solemnly required, and the over-scrupulous observance of it, which,

* John v. 1-16.   † John vii. 19-23.

after all, was simply not required. Taking another view of the subject, if the ritual Law were ordained by God, we cannot believe that our Lord meant, by these actions, indirectly and tacitly to repeal it. A law so solemnly promulgated by God could not be indirectly and tacitly repealed. There is but one other purpose which can be ascribed to his actions. It is, that they were intended, at any risk which the purposes of his mission allowed, to indicate that that Law was not ordained by God, but was a system of human superstition.

We must not refine, in drawing inferences from the words of Jesus, as if they were those of a philosophical treatise, written with great precision, and were not popular language, addressed to rude, unenlightened hearers, with strong prejudices, and incapable of any accurate exercise of intellect. We must regard their essential meaning, and consider the effect obviously intended. But the words used by him at the Feast of Tabernacles, in reference to the facts just mentioned, have a bearing not obvious, perhaps, at first sight, but which, without any violation of the principles just laid down, we cannot well doubt was purposed by our Lord. They have been partly quoted already.

"Did not Moses give you the Law, and yet no one of you regards the Law? Why do you seek to kill me? The crowd answered him; Thou art mad: who seeks to kill thee? Jesus replied to them; I have done one work, at which ye all are astounded. Moses gave you circumcision,—not that it comes from Moses, but from the fathers,—and ye circumcise a child on the Sabbath. If a child be circumcised on the Sabbath, that the Law of Moses may not be broken,\* are ye angry with me for restoring soundness to the whole body of a man on the Sabbath? Judge not according to appearance, but judge righteously."†

Considering the manner in which circumcision is repre-

---

\* As a child, according to the Law, was to be circumcised on the eighth day after its birth, the rite was performed on the Sabbath, if that happened to be the eighth day.
† John vii. 19-24.

sented in the Pentateuch as having been ordained and enforced, there is something well deserving attention in the words in which our Lord first refers it to Moses, and then to the fathers, as if it were, at most, a mere ordinance of Moses, or a traditionary rite of the Jews, sanctioned by him. He does not speak of it as appointed by God. "If a child," he proceeds, " be circumcised on the Sabbath, that the Law of *Moses* may not be broken, are ye angry with *me*," for what I have done? The word "me" is here emphatic. The sentence is antithetical. The question belongs to the class of those passages, in which our Saviour demanded for himself deference like that, or greater than that, which the Jews had been accustomed to pay to those whom they most honoured under their old dispensation; as when he said, "A greater than Solomon is here;"—"Before Abraham existed I was He;"—"Have ye not read what David did?" But, if we follow the Pentateuch in referring the rite mentioned, not to Moses, but to God, as its proper author, the language becomes altogether unsuitable. We shall, at once, perceive this by substituting for "the Law of Moses" an expression corresponding to that conception: "if a child be circumcised on the Sabbath, that the *Law of God* may not be broken, are ye angry with *me?*"—"Are ye angry with me," our Saviour goes on, "for restoring soundness to the whole body of a man?" In these words, the antithesis between the act which he had performed, and the act performed in circumcision, represents the latter, not as a sacred and most important rite, but as a mere mutilation of the body.

The ordinances concerning clean and unclean food form a prominent feature of the ceremonial Law.\* The animals enumerated as unclean were to be an abomination to the Israelites. The touch of their dead bodies was pollution. It rendered even inanimate things unclean. The washing of men, and garments, and vessels, or the breaking of the latter, is enjoined in consequence of it. Minute and extra-

---

\* Leviticus, Ch. xi. Deuteronomy, Ch. xiv.

ordinary directions are given concerning it.* The Jews were not to "make themselves abominable" by eating unclean food; but it is said; "Ye shall sanctify yourselves," by abstaining from such food, "and ye shall be holy, for I, the Lord your God, am holy."

The Pharisees, in the time of our Saviour, attached a most superstitious importance to the washing of the hands before meals.† The custom, probably, originated in the purpose of removing any particle of unclean food that might accidentally adhere to them. Our Saviour was, on one occasion, questioned by the Pharisees on account of the neglect of this ceremony by his disciples.‡ It is unnecessary to give the whole of his reply. He severely reproved them for teaching the commandments of men and making void the commandments of God; with honouring God with their lips, while their hearts were far from Him; and then, turning from the Pharisees, and calling upon the multitude to attend, he said to them;

"Hear and understand! Not that which enters the mouth pollutes a man, but what proceeds from the mouth; it is that which pollutes a man.

"Afterwards his disciples came to him, and said; Do you know that the Pharisees were scandalized, when they heard that speech? But he answered them, Whatever my heavenly Father has not planted [whatever religious doctrine or system of doctrines], is to be rooted up. Leave them to themselves. They are blind leaders of the blind, but when the blind lead the blind, it is to fall headlong. Then Peter said, Explain to us that dark saying;"—meaning the words that our Saviour addressed to the multitude. These were so foreign from the conceptions that the Jews had derived from the Law, that the Apostles did not know how to under-

---

* As, for example; "If any part of such dead body fall upon any sort of seed to be sown, the seed shall be clean, unless, when it fell upon it, the seed had been put in water; for then it shall be unclean to you."—Leviticus xi. 37, 38.
† See Wetstein's note on Matthew xv. 2.
‡ Matthew, Ch. xv. Mark, Ch. vii.

stand them. "And Jesus said, Are ye too still without discernment? Do ye not understand, that what enters the mouth passes into the stomach, and is cast out? But what proceeds from the mouth has its source in the mind, and is that which pollutes a man. For in the mind is the source of evil thoughts, murder, adultery, fornication, theft, false testimony, calumny. These are what pollute a man. But to eat with unwashed hands does not pollute a man."

Perhaps the purpose of the last sentence, in which Jesus recurs to the original occasion of his discourse, was partially to veil from his disciples, as yet unprepared for such full instruction, the whole bearing of the truths he had declared, on the authority of the Levitical Law and the Pentateuch. But their bearing is obvious. They are essential truths of religion. They were uttered by Jesus, as a teacher from God; and they show in what manner he regarded the representations of the Pentateuch concerning clean and unclean animals, and the pollution to be incurred by eating the one, and the holiness to be attained by eating only the other. The fact, that they are in direct opposition to the Levitical Law, is apparent; but it may be made a little more striking to the imagination, if we will conceive of the astounding incongruity that would be produced, were the words of Jesus to be found in Leviticus or Deuteronomy, immediately after the ordinances respecting clean and unclean food.

Christianity is distinguished by the indissoluble sanctity that it attaches to marriage;—strikingly distinguished, when we consider the general licentiousness of principle, as well as practice, among Jews and Heathens, regarding the intercourse of the sexes, which prevailed before the coming of our Saviour. The sacred character with which marriage is invested by our religion is a necessary means of delivering men from the animal selfishness of the appetites, and of educating them as moral and spiritual beings. It transforms the passion of the sexes into a high and generous sentiment, that puts in action and invigorates whatever is noble in our nature. It makes it the foundation of the most intimate friendship. Though the sanctity of marriage has been but imperfectly regarded by Christians, yet its effects have been, to raise woman from the state to which she was degraded by the vices of the ancient world, and is still degraded wherever the influence of Christianity is unknown, and to establish her in her proper rank. It has placed the weaker and more refined portion of our race on an equality with the stronger and ruder, and thus caused the purifying and civilizing influence of female virtue to be everywhere diffused. By making the union of parents indissoluble, it secures to their children care and love. It has infused a new vitality into the ties of natural affection; and these, in their numberless ramifications and interlacings, become the strongest bonds of civil society. It has created domestic life, the close union of individuals into families, the school in which our virtues are now formed in childhood, and the sphere in which our best charities are exercised in maturer years.

But the sanctity of marriage was not recognized in the Levitical Law. It presents in this respect a great contrast with the teaching of Christ. It countenanced the widest liberty of divorce on the part of the husband. If a wife "had not favour in the eyes of her husband, because he had found something offensive in her," he might " write her a bill of divorcement, and put it into her hands, and send her out of his house." * It was in direct opposition to this law (which is, obviously, from the mention of *writing* a bill of divorcement, of an age when writing had become common), that is, it was in direct opposition to the Levitical Law, that our Saviour thus taught;

" It has been said ; Let him who would put away his wife, give her a writing of divorcement. But I say to you, Whoever puts away his wife, except for adultery, causes her to commit adultery ; and whoever marries her who is put away commits adultery."†

In the time of our Saviour, the majority of the Jews inferred, as they were authorized to do, from the Levitical Law,

* Deuteronomy, xxiv. 1.  † Matthew v. 31, 32.

that a man might divorce his wife for any cause of offence whatever. The Pharisees, who had, doubtless, heard something of his teaching respecting this subject, were desirous that it should be brought out in still more open opposition to the Law, that it might afford them an opportunity to excite against him the prejudices of the multitude. They, accordingly, came to question him on the subject, and made their inquiry with a show of deference. The Evangelist thus relates;

"And the Pharisees came to ensnare him, and asked; May a man lawfully divorce his wife for whatever cause he will? And he answered them; Have ye not read, that the Creator, in the beginning, made a male and a female? And it is said; *For this cause shall a man leave his father and his mother, and cleave to his wife; and they two shall be one.* So they are no longer two, but one. What, then, God has joined together, let none put asunder. They said to him, Why, then, has Moses ordained, that a man may give his wife a writing of divorcement, and put her away? He said to them, Moses, on account of your perversity, allowed you to put away your wives; but in the beginning it was not so. And I say to you, that whoever puts away his wife, except for adultery, and marries another, commits adultery; and he who marries her who has been put away commits adultery." *

Here, again, our Saviour directly opposes his teaching to the Levitical Law; not, it should be observed, on the ground that that Law had proceeded from God, but that he was commissioned to revoke it; on the contrary, he declares the Law itself, in the particular in question, essentially bad, and contrary to the will of God. In the words, "Moses, on account of your perversity, allowed you to put away your wives," we are to consider the *essential* idea, which is, that the law had its occasion in the perversity of the Jews. The expression, "Moses allowed," is merely an adaptation of his language to the popular belief, concerning which any direct contro-

* Matthew xix. 3-9.

versy would have defeated the purpose he had in view. But, while using this expression, Jesus, at the same time, affords decisive ground for concluding the belief to be erroneous. If the law respecting divorce proceeded from Moses, it proceeded from God. But a law cannot have proceeded from God which is contrary to the will of God, and accommodated to human perversity; a law that counteracts the moral civilization of men, and indulges them in selfishness, sensuality, and domestic tyranny. It is to be recollected, that the code which contained this law likewise presented a broad contrast to Christianity in sanctioning polygamy and concubinage. How different the teaching of Jesus was from the notions which the Jews had derived from the Levitical Law, and the practice which they had founded upon it, appears from the remark of his own disciples after his conversation with the Pharisees: "If such is the case of a man with his wife, it is better not to marry."

The first mention by Jesus of the Jewish law respecting divorce is found in the Sermon on the Mount. In this discourse the manner is very striking, in which precepts, or principles, derived from the Pentateuch, are introduced to notice, and remarked on by him, for the purpose of extending or contradicting them. His words are; "Ye have heard that it was said to them of old"—"But I say unto you." This is language which cannot be reconciled with the supposition that Jesus held the common belief of his countrymen, that those precepts and principles proceeded immediately from God. Introduce the expression of such a belief, and it would give a strange character to his words; "Ye have heard that God said to them of old"—"But I say to you." Had he intended to sanction the popular belief, and, at the same time, to signify that he was commissioned to enlarge or repeal the laws formerly given by God, we should find some other forms of introduction than those which he has used; as for example, "God spake by Moses to them of old, saying"—"But my Father now says to you."

The argument we are considering has, perhaps, been sufficiently elucidated. But I will add one passage more. It is from the conversation of Jesus with the Samaritan woman, whom he found by Jacob's well.* To her he openly professed himself the Messiah, contrary to the reserve which he was compelled to maintain with the Jews till the closing scenes of his ministry. To her, likewise, he spoke with more plainness in relation to the subject before us. She, believing him to be a prophet, questioned him at once respecting the fundamental point of difference between the Jews and Samaritans; whether God should be worshipped on Mount Gerizim, or at Jerusalem. About the form of worship, which was essentially the same in the temple of the Samaritans and in that of the Jews, there was no question in her mind. But it is to this form of worship that the answer of Jesus relates. "Woman, believe me, the hour is coming when ye shall worship the Father neither on this mountain nor at Jerusalem." I pass over a sentence unimportant to our purpose. "The hour is coming, and now is, when the true worshippers of the Father shall worship him in spirit and truth; for the father is seeking such worshippers. God is a spirit, and they who worship him must worship him in spirit and truth." This passage, viewed in the light in which it has been placed by the preceding inquiry, hardly requires any comment. Those who worshipped, either at Jerusalem or on Mount Gerizim, according to the rites of the Levitical Law, were not such worshippers as God desired. Their religion of ceremonies was not the religion of the heart. Their form of worship was to be done away, as unacceptable to God; and, in contradistinction to them, a new class of men was forming, through the ministry of Christ, who, rejecting all such rites, should worship God spiritually and truly.

We conclude, then, that the tacit and indirect abolition of the ceremonial Law by Christianity, without any claim on the part of Jesus, that, though this law was of divine origin, he was commissioned to repeal it;—the opposition between

* John iv. 5-24.

the spirit and character of our religion, and other portions of the Levitical Law;—and such words and acts of our Saviour as have been mentioned, bearing directly against that Law;—all prove that the popular notions of the Jews respecting its divine origin and authority, and, consequently, their notions respecting the authorship of the Pentateuch, were not sanctioned by him, but were opposed by him as far as a wise regard to the accomplishment of the essential purposes of his ministry would permit.

We will now pass from a consideration of the Pentateuch to some general remarks on the other books of the Old Testament.*

## SECTION VIII.
### ON THE OTHER BOOKS OF THE OLD TESTAMENT BESIDE THOSE OF THE PENTATEUCH.

IN considering the other books of the Old Testament, we must divest ourselves of the Jewish notion of their divine authority; or, in other words, we must divest ourselves of the belief, that the truth of all the facts which they relate, and of all the sentiments which their writers express, rests on the authority of God. When viewed under this aspect, they excite constant objections, and present constant occasions of scandal. But, when they are removed from the false light in which they have been placed, so that their true character may be discerned, we perceive them to be works of the greatest curiosity and interest, coming down to us from a remote antiquity; marking the history of our race with a long track of light, though broken and clouded, where all would be darkness without them; bearing, in their habitual reference to God, which gives them so peculiar a character, the impress of the divine dispensation in which they had their origin; and uttering, with the voice of far distant ages, sentiments of piety to which the heart of man still responds.

* [*See note* E, *at the end of the volume.*—ED.]

In regard to the *miscellaneous* books of the Old Testament, as they may be called, to distinguish them from the historical and prophetical, no further remarks seem necessary with reference to our present purpose. But, respecting the other historical books beside the Pentateuch, the inquiry arises; In what manner should we regard the many accounts of miracles contained in them, and the language which, to a modern reader, at first view, implies the frequent immediate interposition of the Deity in acting upon the minds of men and directing the order of events?

In considering this question, a distinction is to be made among those books. In the Books of Joshua and of Judges, which relate to the period of several centuries, as is commonly supposed, immediately following the settlement of the Jews in Palestine, there is evidently, I conceive, a great mixture of fabulous traditions, such as are found in the early history of all other nations. With the Book of Samuel, the history, to all appearance, assumes a more authentic character;—far more authentic than that of the contemporary history of any other ancient nation; and it continues to preserve a similar character through the Book of Kings. It is these Books of Samuel and of the Kings, that particularly demand attention in further considering the inquiry just presented.

We will first take notice of those forms of expression to be found in them, which refer so much to the immediate agency of the Deity, though without supposing anything properly miraculous, that is, any event not accordant with the ordinary course of nature, that may be recognized as such an event by man. In the occurrences of this world, much, we believe, is left to the free agency of the moral beings who inhabit it; while, on the other hand, religion and philosophy teach us, that much is determined by the unseen operation of the controlling will of God. But to settle the limits of human and divine agency is a problem which no philosophy can solve. However convinced we may be, that man possesses, as essential to all that is excellent in his nature, the power of doing good as his proper act, and consequently the power of doing evil, we are wholly ignorant how far this power is limited and overruled by God's omnipotence. We believe, as the necessary ground-work of religion and morals, that God, though the ultimate, is not the immediate, cause of all events; and that a wide distinction is to be made between what He directly ordains, and what He permits. But this distinction was overlooked by the Jewish historians. Accustomed to the habitual contemplation of God as the author of all things, deeply penetrated by a sense of the marvellous circumstances under which their nation existed, and regarding it as the object of his special providence, they naturally referred *directly* to Him whatever affected its condition, and whatever seemed to them a manifestation of his pleasure or displeasure. This state of mind they, of course, shared with their countrymen. We have scarcely entered on the Book of Samuel, before we find it related, that " the elders of Israel said, Wherefore hath the Lord smitten us to-day before the Philistines?" * The same mode of conception and style of narration appear throughout the history. To remark on one of the passages, by which the early fathers were embarrassed, it is said, that " an evil spirit, from the Lord, troubled Saul."† A modern historian might express the same event by saying, that Saul became subject to temporary insanity. A religious man, if he wished to present the fact under a religious aspect, would now say, that in the providence of God Saul was thus afflicted. The last mode of expression would differ from that used by the Jewish historian, not only in putting aside the agency of an evil spirit, but also in not *directly* referring the effect to God. It is to be kept in mind, that in all such language throughout the Jewish history, we have only an expression of the conceptions of the writer. Of the counsels of God he could know nothing.

The next branch of the inquiry is; In what manner we are to regard the accounts of miracles contained in the Books of Samuel and of the Kings. The Book of the Kings, as

---

\* 1 Samuel iv. 3.  † 1 Samuel xvi. 14.

has been formerly remarked, was written, or compiled, after the commencement of the Babylonish Captivity. It begins with an account of the last days of David. Between the composition of the history and the first events related in it, was an interval, therefore, of more than four centuries and a half. It has been supposed by many, that the Book of Samuel was originally united with that of the Kings, as forming one work by the same author. But it seems to me most probable, that they are different works by different authors, and I shall continue to speak of them as such. The Book of Samuel has been thought, from internal evidence, to have been written a considerable time after the conclusion of the series of historical events which it records, and these events extend through a period of about a hundred and fifty years.

In the Books of Samuel and of the Kings, we find many accounts of supposed miracles, in the proper sense of the word. In regard to such accounts, we must recollect, that we are wholly ignorant of the writer of either work; that, consequently, we know nothing concerning either writer to justify any peculiar confidence in his habits of investigation, his judgment, or his trustworthiness; that neither of them gave his testimony under personal circumstances that might tend to confirm it; that each of them wrote so long after many or most of the events which he narrates, that tradition might have done her common work in introducing fables, and changing natural events into marvels; and that both of them lived in that stage of civilization in which men are prone to the belief of the supernatural, and among a people in whom this tendency had been especially strengthened. The miracles by which the dispensation of Moses was confirmed, whatever they were, must have been such as deeply to affect the imaginations of the Israelites. It is the necessary consequence of a miraculous dispensation, to render men's minds familiar with the idea of the special manifestation of divine power, and to dispose them for a long time to acquiesce in the belief of supposed instances of such a manifestation. The case may naturally have been the same with the miracles of Moses, as it was with those of Christ and his Apostles. The former, as well as the latter, may have given occasion to many accounts of false miracles, such as we find in the works of the Christian fathers, particularly of the later fathers. There is nothing to render it probable that the writers of the Jewish nation were less likely to fall into error than those of the Christian church. While no one, who puts aside the notion of the divine authority of all the books of the ancient Hebrews, can doubt, that extravagant fables and false prodigies are found in all those relating to that portion of their history which precedes the time of Samuel, while the whole history of the ancient world is full of pretended marvels, there seems no reason to except the Books of Samuel and of the Kings as free from this mixture. These views of the subject, it may seem, will justify us in rejecting altogether the accounts of miracles which they contain.

I think not. There is a different view to be taken. The considerations suggested will, undoubtedly, justify us in rejecting without hesitation all such accounts as clearly appear to us to imply wrong conceptions of God, and in regarding others, of not so marked a character, with great scepticism. But those considerations have no bearing on another question that arises; Whether it were possible, that the great end for which the Jews were preserved a separate people could have been accomplished, had there been no other miracles attesting the peculiar relation of that people to God, than those which accompanied their separation by Moses. When we recollect, that they were a small people surrounded by an idolatrous world, and often lapsing into idolatry themselves; when we recollect, that we are looking back to a period of history, when the idea of God, in its rudest form, was unknown to the generality of men, we may well doubt, whether a succession of miracles was not necessary to preserve it among the Jews. But, were this the case, there is no presumption against their occurrence. On the contrary, we must believe that the necessary means were used by God to effect the purpose intended by Him. I am reasoning throughout, as is apparent, without reference to that philosophy, as shallow, in my view, as it is irreligious, according to which God is bound by his own wisdom, or by some other necessity of his nature, not to manifest himself to men for any end whatever, except through those operations of his power which we call the laws of nature.

Believing, then, that God may have wrought miracles among the Israelites subsequently to the time of Moses, we shall find in their historical books some accounts which there seems little reason to question, Let us turn, for example, to the eighteenth chapter of the first Book of Kings. Amid the general idolatry of the kingdom of Israel under Ahab, after the slaughter, by Jezebel, of the prophets of the Lord, Elijah appears from his retirement, to present himself before the king. "And when Ahab saw Elijah he said, Art thou he who troubles Israel? And Elijah answered, I have not troubled Israel, but thou and thy father's house, in forsaking the commandments of Jehovah and following false gods." The whole demeanour of the persecuted prophet corresponds to this fearless expression of high and unshrinking dignity. He demands an assembly of the people, before whom the many hundreds of the prophets of Baal, and of the groves, should meet him alone. In the presence of the assembled nation, he appeals to God for his decision: "Lord! God of Abraham, Isaac, and Israel, Hear me, O Lord! hear me, that this people may know, that thou the Lord art God. Then the fire of the Lord fell, and consumed the sacrifice, and the wood, and the stones, and the earth, and licked up the water that was in the trench."

The credibility of this account is confirmed by the essential importance of the occasion on which this miracle is said to have been performed, when the religion of God was trampled down by a persecuting idolatry. It is confirmed by the extraordinary publicity asserted for it as wrought in the presence of an assembled people, during a period of authentic history. But the noble presentation of moral grandeur in the situation and character of the prophet, and the transcendent magnificence of the description, vivid with all the marks of truth, are alone, perhaps, sufficient to create a presumption of the reality of the event, scarcely less strong than their immediate effect on the imagination and feelings. More, however, than all this, we have the most solemn attestation to the fact, that Elijah was a special messenger of God. In the Transfiguration of our Saviour, Elijah appeared in company with Moses, as associated with Jesus. Elijah, then, was a prophet of God; and, as a prophet of God, his mission had been sealed by miracles; and what miracle can we imagine more suited to his character, as a teacher and restorer of true religion among the idolatrous Israelites, than that described by the historian? *

These considerations, however, do not prove, that all which is related concerning Elijah is to be received as it is told. I have before remarked, that the occurrence of real miracles has a tendency to give rise to false reports of miracles, and to procure credit for such stories. Counterfeit coin circulates with the true. It is a very striking proof of the authenticity and genuineness of the Gospels, that, among the many narratives which they contain of miracles performed by Jesus, there are none, the intrinsic character of which may suggest a well-grounded doubt of their credibility. It is an equally striking evidence of the authority which these books obtained from the beginning, that they thoroughly checked the growth of all fabulous narratives of miracles as wrought by him during his ministry. It is only a confirmation of the force of this argument, that a crop of fabulous marvels relating to his infancy and childhood, of which some seed seems to have been early scattered, sprung up after the fourth century, and flourished during the dark ages. These fables are still to be found in the Gospels of the Infancy, and other books of the same class, and some of them in the Koran.

In regard to the history of the Jews, I believe that the concerns of that nation, like those of all other nations and individuals, were under the special providence of God; by which term, sometimes abused,—as what term of religion has not been?—I mean an agency of God that is undis-

---

* [See note F, at the end of the volume.—ED.]

cernible by man in the particular instances of its operation, which is apart from, and, if I may so speak, lies behind, the ordinary concatenation of causes and effects, that alone falls under our cognizance, and which veils it from our view; but an agency by which the condition of God's creatures in this world is continually affected. Beside this special providence, we have seen what reasons there are for believing that miracles, subsequent to those of Moses, made a part of the Jewish dispensation. This fact is not only consistent with the supposition, that in the Jewish books of history there are many accounts of miracles not to be credited, but, considering all the circumstances under which those books were composed, it would naturally lead us, before examination, to anticipate that such would be the case. The conclusion, that in the Jewish histories there are many accounts of miracles not to be credited, has no bearing whatever on our religious faith, our morals, or our happiness, except one that is very important; it relieves the mind from all the perplexity, confusion, and religious scepticism, produced by the inconsistency of those accounts with just conceptions of the Divinity.

After what has been said, it is, perhaps, scarcely necessary to observe, that there is nothing in the character of the Jewish historians to qualify them to be guides in religion or morals. On these subjects they shared in the rude and erroneous notions of their countrymen, which were far in advance of those of the heathen world, but far behind those of an enlightened Christian. We are not called upon to adopt their moral judgments, expressed or implied, respecting characters or actions. Nor is it improbable, that they, or the earlier relators whom they followed, were influenced in their representations by personal or party prejudices. These remarks may seem to some too obvious to be thus formally stated; but we are not a century removed from the time, when the credibility of revelation was thought to be involved in the proof, that David was *a man after God's own heart*, because the anonymous author of the Book of Samuel represents Samuel as using this expression concerning him.

We pass to the prophetical books. The prophets were the public religious teachers of the Jews. This was their distinguishing characteristic. The true prophets conscientiously addressed their countrymen as ministers of God. It was their business to instruct, warn, threaten, exhort, and encourage the people.

These were the true prophets; but the name "prophet" was equally extended to those who dishonestly, and with bad purposes, assumed the character of teachers of the national religion. Thus we find mention of false prophets as well as true. It was given to those also who taught the worship of idols, as we read, for instance, of the prophets of Baal. The leading idea to be formed of a prophet is that of a public religious teacher, whether honest or dishonest, whether the professed minister of the true God or of some false god. In our own language the word "prophet" is now restricted to denoting, in its proper sense, one miraculously commissioned to foretell events. It is too late to change the name as applied to the Jewish teachers; but if we would avoid error we must give it the additional meaning just explained. It would be a great extravagance to suppose that all those called prophets in the Old Testament were regarded as possessing the miraculous power of foretelling events, or as making pretensions to this power.

The prophets whose writings remain, in addressing the Jewish people, often insisted on the certain or probable consequences of their sins; on impending dangers, which could be avoided only, if at all, by a return to their duty; on the blessings which would follow reformation and goodness; on the mercy of God as about to be displayed in some approaching deliverance; and on that constant faith which the Jews, as his chosen people, might repose on his providence, if obedient to his will. It is the office of every teacher of religion and virtue to look to the future, and to point out the consequences of conduct. The imaginations of the prophets were strongly affected by a sense of the connection of the Jewish nation with God. They described this connection in the strongest terms. They spoke of the nation in a figure hardly agreeable to our ears, when we suffer the mind to dwell upon it, as *God's inheritance*, or peculiar possession. Viewing it as existing through its past and anticipated history, they personified it as Israel, *his servant, his son, the child whom he had loved,* who might be chastised for the sins of a particular generation, but whose enemies and oppressors were to be destroyed, and for whom a future glory, as yet unknown, was in reserve. Thus their writings often assumed the form of prediction. The prophets, also, as ministers of God, were accustomed, with the licensed boldness of oriental poetry, to introduce God as through themselves addressing the people, and to represent their declarations of what they believed conformable to his will and purposes, as immediately suggested by him. Their language in these respects, though different in the turn of expression, was the same, in meaning and effect, with that which has been uttered from Christian pulpits down to our own time; and that which every religious and moral teacher may or must use when he believes himself to be stating what is indisputably the law of God.

It is clear that there is much in the language, conceptions, and sentiments of the authors of the prophetical books (so called), which is not to be referred directly to God; and so far as we have proceeded in our remarks on them, we may proceed with assurance. But there are good reasons for entertaining the question, Whether some of their number were not occasionally employed as ministers of God under his immediate direction, and endued with the power of predicting events directly revealed to them by Him. In the supposition that they were so, there is nothing intrinsically incredible; and such may have been the fact, even though no conclusive evidence of it now remain. We cannot expect to be able to ascertain all that has taken place in the extraordinary, any more than in the ordinary, manifestations of God. But the question, as regards our own belief, is simply, Whether we have sufficient evidence of the truth of this supposition, or whether the balance of probabilities inclines for or against it. In the opinion which has commonly prevailed relating to this subject, much has been assumed without proof; there has been a great want of critical inquiry, and of logical and well-founded reasoning. On the other hand, the opinion directly opposed to it has been rested chiefly on a principle, destructive of any belief in revelation, and of any religious sentiment toward God as a personal being, or rather of any belief in the God of Christianity; I mean the principle, that rejects all extraordinary interpositions of God, and regards the power that governs the universe as capable only of a sort of mechanical action;—God and matter being equally controlled by certain inevitable laws, the Laws of Nature.

The subject deserves a much more thorough and judicious examination than it has received; an examination to be carried through successfully only by one who unites the qualifications of a true Christian philosopher, a wide thinker, an able reasoner, an enlightened critic, and a laborious and accurate scholar. Its result might, perhaps, attain a high degree of probability. It might at least present us with all that can now be known on the subject. But in the mean time, if our opinions must remain more or less uncertain, it is an uncertainty that in no way affects our virtue or happiness.

The direct evidences of the divine authority of our religion have been divided into miracles and prophecies. But it is obvious, that a prophecy is only a miracle of a particular kind, and that, however clear and satisfactory, it can carry with it no particular proof, different from that afforded by any other miracle. In order that a prophecy may be received as evidence, its supernatural character must be unquestionable. There must be no doubt respecting either its meaning, or its correspondence with the event predicted, or its intended reference to that event. There must be no mode of accounting for the correspondence between the prophecy and the event, except by referring the former to the omniscience of God. These conditions are not, as I conceive, fulfilled by those passages of the Old Testament which have been alleged as prophecies of Jesus. The Jews, interpreting the Old Testament allegorically, had applied many passages in it to their expected Messiah. A portion of the disciples of Jesus (apparently not all) retained the common notions of their countrymen respecting this subject, and we accordingly find some of those passages applied to Him in the Gospel of Matthew, the Acts of the Apostles, and the Epistle to the Hebrews. In what is reported concerning the conversations of our Saviour, there are some expressions that may require explanation;* but he never appeals in evidence of his divine mission to any words of a Jewish prophet, as containing a miraculous prediction.

The writers of the prophetical books undoubtedly believed, that the series of God's dispensations to their nation was not completed; that something greater was in reserve for it; that all the marvellous preparation which had been made was to produce other results than what had yet taken place. This belief gathered strength in after times. The chosen people, harassed and subjugated, could not but look forward to some miraculous interposition, by which God would at last manifest his purposes toward them and toward the world. They were expecting the appearance of that great minister, by whom those purposes would be accomplished— the Anointed One, the Messiah. This messenger came. The object of his coming was unlike what they had anticipated; the kingdom which he was to establish was not that which they had looked for; the results, as regarded their own nation, were altogether different. But he was the long-expected Messiah, the Anointed One of God. He had come to fulfil the purpose of the Jewish dispensation. Our Saviour accomplished not any express prophecy relating to him, but he came in conformity to an expectation, which the whole tenor of God's providence toward their nation had taught the Jews to entertain.

The main purpose of these remarks on the books treated of in this Section, as well as of those on the Pentateuch, has

* I have formerly adverted to this subject in an article published in "The Christian Examiner," Vol. v. for 1828, pp. 53-59.

been to show, that these writings, when their character is properly understood, afford no ground of objection to the Jewish or Christian dispensation. But the subject suggests some other reflections, to which we will attend in the next Section.

## SECTION IX.

### *Concluding Remarks upon the Old Testament.*

IN one of the most popular of the works introductory to the books of the Old Testament, written by a late prelate of the Church of England, they are spoken of as forming "that consecrated canon, in which the holy oracles were preserved by the Jews, which was stamped as infallible by the testimony of Christ and his apostles, and which, in the first and purest ages of the church, was reverenced (together with the inspired books of the New Testament) as the only source of revealed wisdom." *

Such, in conformity with the creeds of different churches and sects, has been the language of many theologians respecting the Old Testament. They have represented it as having proceeded miraculously from God himself, the human writers being agents of the Divine Mind, in the same manner as a divine origin has been ascribed by the Hindoos to their Vedas and other sacred books, by the Mahometans to the Koran, and by the Parsees to the Zend-Avesta. They have, in consequence, received the accounts, given in its different books, of the Deity, of his acts, and of his communications to the Israelites, as constituting a revelation which He has made of his character. They have regarded the moral judgments which those writings express or imply, as conformed to the highest standard of benevolence and justice, and as affording the most authoritative directions for our own conduct. And they have viewed all the events

---

* Gray's Key to the Old Testament, Preface.

related, however legendary some of them may appear, as not only possible but certain; and, so far as they pretend to a supernatural character, as altogether worthy of God. At the same time they have rejected those expedients by which the early catholic Christians modified their belief, and attempted to reconcile it with the actual character of the books of the Old Testament.

When we compare the modern, unqualified doctrine concerning those books, with that more complex one held by the generality of the early Christians, on the one hand, or with the opinion of the Gnostics, on the other, it is not easy to say which of the three is most irrational. We marvel at ancient errors; for our wonder has not been deadened by familiarity; but false doctrines prevail in our own time, which, if we were a little further removed from their sphere, would appear to us not less amazing. The history of opinions concerning religion comprehends the whole history of the most portentous absurdities, and the most pernicious errors, into which mankind have fallen. In the history of Christian theology, we find these errors and absurdities clustering round the essential truths of religion, concealing them from view, and counteracting and annihilating their influence. We cannot here inquire into all the causes which have produced this state of things; but we may observe, that one occasion of the prevalence of error, and of the obstinacy with which it has been maintained, is to be found in the essential character of religion itself.

The truths of religion relate to our spiritual nature, to the government of God, to the unseen world, to eternity, to the Infinite Being. Now these are all subjects which, in many of their aspects and relations, not only lie beyond the limits of our knowledge, but transcend our power of comprehension. We cannot, for instance, grasp the idea of infinity; we can only conceive of it negatively, as the absence of all limitation. Of propositions concerning it, directly contradictory, we can neither affirm nor deny one nor the other. Who will say, that created things may or may not have existed from eternity? Who will affirm, that creation does not imply a commencement of existence? Who will maintain, that the power of creation has not always been an attribute of the Deity, and may not from eternity have been exercised by Him? Who will say, that the universe does or does not exist within circumscribed limits, surrounded on all sides by an infinite expanse of void space? Who will contend, on the one hand, that things finite and bounded in their nature must not lie within definite bounds; or, on the other hand, that there are definite bounds beyond which God has not manifested, and cannot manifest, his power and goodness? In attempting to answer consistently questions concerning subjects like these, our reason finds a barrier which it cannot pass. Nor are these the only, nor the most interesting, class of questions respecting the objects of religion, which require for their solution other knowledge, or other powers, than what we possess. The consideration of such questions may teach us, that it is an important part of our wisdom, "to know how little can be known;" to

"Wait the great teacher, Death, and God adore."

To a being of a higher order, how incongruous must it appear, that man,—a creature just formed; but a short while ago a helpless infant, or an ignorant child; whose imperfect faculties are the growth of a few years; whose understanding is so liable to be deceived by the errors of others, and perverted by the meaner part of his own nature; who so often errs in judgment concerning the objects immediately around him; whose knowledge of the Creation, its past history through illimitable time, and its inexhaustible modes of being through illimitable space, is that of a stranger just introduced into it, just learning its language, and confined to a circuit of a few miles,—that man, so very ignorant and incapable, should undertake to solve the problem of the Universe, and to discuss, as if the subject lay all within his comprehension, the character, counsels, and works of the Infinite Being. The essential truths of religion we know, for they have been taught us by God through Christ, and this knowledge is of inestimable value; but beyond and around them is a region into which we cannot penetrate. Yet this region men have attempted to explore, and have returned from it with their reason so baffled and confounded, as to be incapable of discerning the real character of familiar objects, and comprehending the true meaning of words. In this state of mind they have come to the examination of subjects, related to their faith, of which the human understanding is fully cognizant. Finding, that in the nature of things there were problems connected with religion which they could not solve, they have been ready to acquiesce in verbal or moral absurdities concerning it, the fictions of human folly, as if the latter were of the same character with the former. But true philosophy will teach us to keep in mind the limits of those powers which God has given us, equally in respect to what lies within our capacity, as what lies beyond it.

The error that has been committed in representing the books of the Old Testament as of divine origin and authority, or, in other words, as constituting an essential part of a revelation from God, which error, of course, involves the belief, that it is a fundamental doctrine of religion so to regard those books, has, beyond question, been a most serious hindrance to all rational belief of the fact, that God has miraculously revealed Himself to man,—the fact of incomparably the most interest in the history of our race. It is this fact which connects man with God, and the present life with the unseen and eternal. By introducing the supernatural into the natural world it unites them into one system, and changes the aspect of all things around us, spreading over them a light from Heaven. The immediate action of the Deity intervening in the course of human affairs, has brought the proofs of religion fully within the scope of our comprehension and powers of reasoning. Every one may understand the evidences of Christianity. And it is the revelation that God has made of Himself by Christianity, which presents the overpowering and unfathomable idea of the Infinite Spirit under those aspects in which alone it may be comprehended by us. It brings God to our view in his relations to man, as the Father of the Universe. To a Christian, religion is not a subject of "lawless and uncertain thoughts," bewildered in the mazes of speculation. Revelation has given fixedness to his conceptions of God, of immortality, and of responsibility. It has exhibited the objects of religion in their proper relation to the things of this life, and invested them with their true character, as the most solemn of realities; while without it the shadows of this world, as our years pass away, assume shapes more and more fearful.

It is on Christianity, as a miraculous revelation, that religion must rest as its principal and only safe support. If Jesus Christ spoke with authority from God, attested by supernatural displays of God's power, we need look for no further evidence of all that is essential to our faith,—of all that is essential to our happiness as spiritual and immortal beings. But if we reject Christianity, we cannot fall back even on the uncertainty which preceded it in the Pagan world; for this uncertainty is rendered darker and more gloomy by the supposition, that God (or the Power, whatever it may be, that acts throughout the Universe) has left the most enlightened portion of mankind to found their religious hopes on a delusion, and by the consequent distrust, which must necessarily be produced, in all the efforts of man's reason to attain any satisfactory conclusions respecting the objects of religion.

It is to Christianity, then, that we must look as the main source of human improvement and happiness. It is in her cause that the battle between good and evil is to be fought. But, in order that we may successfully maintain our religion, we must have a clear conception of what it is, and of what it is not. Pure Christianity is pure religion and pure morality; but what characterizes it as Christianity is, that it rests the evidence of the truths essential to the virtue and happiness of man on the attestation of God; and that in the very fact which it supposes of his miraculous interposition,—that in this fact alone, it affords a most glorious exemplification and proof of the truths which it teaches concerning his paternal character, and his purposes towards us. But, under the much-abused name of Christianity, superstition has sheltered great errors, doctrines alien from its spirit, contradictory to its essential truths, revolting to reason, and even doctrines utterly outraging justice and humanity,—the doctrines of religious tyranny and persecution. Many of these errors, embodied in the creeds of churches and sects, and in the decrees of councils, still burden the Christian world. It is to their public renunciation, however distant the period of it may be, that we must look for any great improvement in the moral and religious condition of men. Then the force of the evidences of our faith may be far more widely recognized, and its proper influence, uncounteracted by those errors, may be far more generally felt. But, in the mean time, there is for every one a consideration which even more intimately concerns him. The more correct are his own conceptions of Christianity, and the more strong is his own conviction of its truth, the greater power will it have to elevate his character; to enable him to live wisely and honourably, and, if no severe trials be appointed him, happily; to make him useful to those he loves, and to all whom he may serve; and to prepare him for that higher state of being, of which Christianity alone can give him any assurance.

# NOTES.

### Note A. page 29.

Ewald (*Die Psalmen*, p. 236) thinks it not improbable, that in this passage there *is* an allusion to the Pentateuch, and that the poet speaks of himself as going into the Temple with this holy book in his hand. But then Ewald assigns to the psalm a comparatively recent date, in the time between the religious reform in the reign of Josiah, on the discovery of a copy of the Law in the Temple, and the Exile—a period which he calls the first golden age of the written law, before it was exposed to the corruptions and abuses of a later day. This unknown author, to whom he ascribes several other psalms, he supposes to have witnessed the destruction of Jerusalem, and to have lived into the period of the Exile. The adoption, therefore, of Ewald's interpretation of these words would not materially affect the argument for a *late* origin of the Pentateuch, though it would imply its existence before the Exile. But his assumption that the "Book-roll" here mentioned is the Pentateuch is wholly gratuitous, and unsupported by any proof. Neither Hitzig nor De Wette adopt his view. The former, who ascribes the psalm to Jeremiah, thinks there is allusion to a roll of that prophet's oracles. The latter paraphrases the whole verse thus: "I approach thee with the teachings of thy law written on my heart"—referring for illustration to Jeremiah xxxi. 33.

### Note B. page 35.

It may be proper to state that a great authority on Hebrew history, Ewald (*Gesch. des Volkes Israel*, i. pp. 215-254), differs in some degree from De Wette and Mr. Norton in this estimate of the Book of Chronicles. He thinks that, with the Books of Ezra and Nehemiah, it formed part of a late Universal History, of which Jerusalem was the central object—a Jerusalem-Chronicle as he calls it—written, probably, at the commencement of Greek ascendancy—perhaps in the age of Alexander the Great; and that it contains many curious and instructive notices of earlier times, derived from sources now lost, and furnished nowhere else. He admits, however, that it is distinguished by a strong *sacerdotal* tendency throughout, and that it presents, in this respect, a marked contrast to the *prophetic* spirit of the Books of Samuel and Kings; and from the importance which it attaches to the Levitical musical services, he conjectures that its author may have been one of the choristers attached to the Temple. Some other recent critics agree with Ewald in this more favourable judgment of the historical character of Chronicles, and in thinking that we are indebted to it for some valuable supplementary matter derived from ancient and authentic sources, and not contained in the earlier books: Bertheau (*Die Bücher der Chronik erklärt. Einleit.* p. xliv.); Bleek (*Einleit. A. T.* p. 399); Movers (*Krit. Untersuch. über bibl. Chron.*) quoted by Bleek. Even De Wette, in the last edition of his *Einleit. A. T.*, has somewhat qualified the harshness of his original censure, and allows that many reliable statements may be found in it (§ 191). Notwithstanding these concessions, Mr. Norton's main position still holds good; that when the accounts in Chronicles are at variance with those of the earlier books, especially in passages which tend to the exaltation of the Levitical caste—they are entitled to no weight.

NOTE C. PAGE 45.

The statement in the text is put in too unqualified a form. Scholars of high name have maintained that the Hebrews were acquainted with alphabetical characters as early as the time of Moses. Eichhorn, who regarded the Pentateuch as substantially Mosaic, has attempted to show that convenient implements and materials for writing existed already in that age, and this opinion he retained, in the main unaltered after forty years, in the latest editions of his work (*Einleit. A. T.*, 1823, § 405). Ewald, arguing from the use of the same terms connected with the art of writing in all the branches of the Semitic tongue, thinks that some very ancient Semitic tribe had acquired the use of the art before the historical age, and that from their brethren of this stock, and not from the Egyptians, the Hebrews learned it during their residence in Egypt: and he ventures on the supposition, that the oldest historians of Israel found a mass of written materials belonging to the Semitic tribes already prepared to their hands (*Gesch. des Volkes Israel*, i. p. 66 *seq.*) Mr. Kenrick is of opinion, that during the close union of Phœnicia with Egypt, in the time of the Hyksos, the alphabetical character of the former was arranged, and learned by the Israelites; but that the art, though known to this latter people at the time of the Exodus, was little diffused among the nation at large. He thinks that an adaptation of the Egyptian phonetic system was more likely to have been made by Phœnicians than by Jews, and that their use of the same alphabet is best explained by their dwelling together in Egypt, before they were neighbours in Canaan (*Ancient Egypt*, ii. p. 324). Mr. Sam. Sharpe, whose eminence as an Egyptologist, entitles him to speak with authority, has no doubt that the Egyptians, many centuries before Moses, were acquainted with the use of alphabetical characters, and that consequently the Israelites could have had no difficulty in learning the use of an alphabet in Egypt.—Nevertheless, the remarkable uniformity of character which marks the language of all the extant literature of the ancient Hebrews, seems to show that in its actual form it must have been produced within a comparatively limited period,—between the age of David and Solomon, or at least of Samuel, and the centuries immeditaely following the Captivity; and that if earlier writings once existed, they have all perished. It is difficult to meet the force of Mr. Norton's reasonings on this point. The perpetuity of form in some languages, as the Greek subsequent to the Alexandrine age, and the rabbinical Hebrew, is not a parallel case. It was the result of a widely-diffused practice of writing among classes of men devoted to literary composition, with classical models constantly before their eyes, and under all the restraints of a strictly-defined grammatical system—suppositions which are wholly irreconcilable with the social condition of the centuries which preceded the Davidian era.

NOTE D. PAGE 70.

Mr. Norton has anticipated on this passage (Exod. xxi. 20, 21) the objection which caused such a "revulsion of feeling" in the mind of Dr. Colenso's intelligent Zulu convert; and in its remoter effects wrought such a change in the views of the honest bishop himself, as ultimately "snapped in twain altogether the cord which had hitherto bound him to the ordinary belief in the historical veracity of the Pentateuch" (*Pentateuch and Book of Joshua*, ch. i. 2nd edit. p. 9).

NOTE E. PAGE 111.

In spite of the plausible reasoning employed by Mr. Norton in this seventh section, many will perhaps feel it more consistent with the grand simplicity and truthfulness of Christ's character, to suppose that he shared the general belief of his country and his age respecting the Mosaic origin and generally divine authority of the Law—deficient as that belief clearly was in precision and even in perfect self-consistency—than to impute to him a mental reservation which left his interior conviction at variance with his habitual language. The case of the retention of a popular phraseology, after science has demonstrated its incorrectness, is not to the point; for such phraseology has no connection with moral and religious ideas. It involves no distinction between an esoteric and an exoteric doctrine. Whereas the notions about the Law and the Prophets, demoniacal possession, a personal devil and other matters, which Christ's words, taken in their obvious sense, clearly favour—formed a part of the popular belief of Palestine, which it was Christ's special mission to act upon and kindle into a more earnest life. The divine authority of the Law and the Prophets is assumed as the basis of the Sermon on the Mount. They are only spiritualized into a new significance. All great prophets in every age have sympathized deeply with popular beliefs and feelings, except in the one point where they aimed at special reformation. Such sympathy is even a condition of prophetic efficiency. It brings it home to the popular heart. It distinguishes it from the intellectual action of the philosophical teacher. In regard to Christ, the language of the New Testament only leaves us the alternative between the admission of some intellectual limitation on the human side of his being, which brought him into living contact with his countrymen,—or the supposition of a certain moral duplicity on the side of it, which connected him with God. What he actually said, we have no means of knowing, except from what is recorded. To assume in Christ, *à priori*, intellectual completeness, and wherever any statement occurs at war with that assumption, to get rid of it by supposing the record defective or mistaken, is surely an abuse of the rationalizing process applied to Scripture, which can only lead to the most arbitrary treatment of its text. Mr. Norton has well argued that we ought not to demand from the writers of the Gospel narrative the clear and well-defined ideas of our modern theology and philosophy. Is it reasonable, when we consider his work and the conditions of it, to expect them from Christ himself?

NOTE F. PAGE 117.

Mr. Norton's position, that God cannot be controlled by his own laws (p. 116), or rather, to speak more correctly, that there may be laws in the spiritual universe deeper and broader than those which govern the material world, and which we call the " Laws of Nature,"— is undoubtedly true, and the necessary postulate of all sound religious philosophy. But his selection of a passage from the history of Elijah, as an illustration of the miraculous in the Old Testament, " which there seems little reason to question," is singularly unfortunate and destructive of the force of his own reasoning. In the whole compass of the Old Testament there is hardly a narrative more obviously legendary in its character than the magnificent episode of Elijah and Elisha. It breaks through the ordinary prose of the accompanying history, like a sudden outburst of the grandest religious poetry. It evidently embodied a tradition from the old and fearful time, when the worships of Jehovah and Baal were struggling for ascendancy in the northern kingdom; and it must be confessed, that it is darkly tinged with the ferocious spirit of religious intolerance and extermination which belonged to the age. It was hardly candid in Mr. Norton to pass over so completely in silence the note which immediately follows the account of the miracle, than which " he can imagine none more suited to the character of a teacher and restorer of true religion:" (1 Kings xviii. 38–40.) " And Elijah said unto them, take the prophets of Baal; let not one of them escape. And they took them: and Elijah brought them down to the brook Kishon, and slew them there." The massacre of four hundred and fifty men, the ignorant and unconscious devotees of a false worship, was the sequel of a transaction which, we are told, signalized Elijah as a true prophet of God, "whose mission had been sealed by miracles." Charlemagne's treatment of the recusant Saxons found a precedent in this bloody and merciless deed. Mr. Norton, it is true, adds that not "all which is related concerning Elijah is to be received as it is told." But can anything be more unreasonable than this arbitrary rejection of a portion of the narrative, because it contains what our moral feelings do not approve? Such a mode of interpretation would hand over the text of the Bible to the uncontrolled wilfulness of everyone's subjective feeling, or fancy. The narrative is a self-consistent whole throughout, and the sequel is in perfect harmony with its general character. But we are not left to this internal evidence alone, for showing that the end of the transaction is as much entitled to credit as what precedes it. We learn from the ensuing history, that in this terrible religious war the example of Elijah was not without effect on the conduct of the Jehovists against their adversaries. Jehu, who subverted the idolatrous dynasty of Ahab, was summoned by Elijah and anointed by Elisha to the kingly office, and took a very decided part in the effort to establish the worship of Jehovah. What means he thought lawful for the accomplishment of that end, we gather from 2 Kings x. 18-28. He did not shrink from perjury and blasphemy. He enticed the worshippers of Baal from all Israel to a solemn religious festival, and the more effectually to conceal his design, offered up with his own hands a sacrifice to the false god; and then let in his emissaries whom he had previously stationed in the vicinity of the temple, to slaughter the unsuspecting worshippers. His order was, "If any of the men whom I have brought into your hands escape, it shall be life for life." "Thus," adds the historian, "did Jehu destroy Baal out of Israel."

It is impossible to apply the outward test of miracle, as the authentic sign of a direct commission from God, in so mixed a history as that of the Israelites, without making the All-holy and the All-merciful responsible for some acts, on which we could not look without a shuddering reprobation in his creatures. Is it not at once a safer and more reverent course, to let the eternal truths and sublime aspirations which are peculiar to the Hebrew prophets, and could only come to them from God, shine with their own divine light in the midst of the human passions and infirmities through which they reveal themselves, and carry the witness of their origin and authority with them to the hearts of the pious in every age,—instead of demanding as the sole evidence of true prophecy, some outward and visible sign of supernatural power, which extends its sanction beyond particular words and acts to the whole character and agency of which they form a part, and which, however we may explain their occurrence in a far distant past, and whatever may have been their effect on contemporaries, have proved, as used by theologians, a constant puzzle and stumbling-block to posterity, and weakened more faith than they have confirmed?